No More Darkness
Only Victory!

Raelene Hudson

Perfect Partner Publishing

Dedication

This book is dedicated to my family. My parents, who taught me to always put God first and to love others the way Christ loves us. My husband, who loves me and allows me to be who God created me to be. My children, who stretch me to move out of my comfort zone and follow God's will.

I want to give special thanks to my son, Garris Hudson. Without him this book would not have been possible. I also want to thank my daughter, Kaitlyn Hudson Dinger, who helped edit and is one of my biggest supporters and encouragers. Kristin Stewart, my dearest friend, who helped edit and loves me the way Jesus desires. Mary Smith and Penny Anderson, my dear friends, who helped with the final editing process. The cover would not have been possible without the creative talents of Grady Truitt. I also want to thank Pastor Larry for his continual leadership and encouragement in my life. His messages of God's truth have continually challenged me to step out in faith and bring God glory! Finally, I want to thank Jesus who gives us life abundantly and who promises to never leave us nor forsake us.

continually challenged me to step out in faith and bring God glory! Finally, I want to thank Jesus who gives us life abundantly and who promises to never leave us nor forsake us.

Contents

Introduction	1
Chapter 1: What is Darkness?	7
Chapter 2: What is Light?	13
Chapter 3: Hearing the Voice of God!	19
Chapter 4: Seeking Wisdom!	25
Chapter 5: The Word of God!	33
Chapter 6: Embracing the Truth!	39
Chapter 7: Recognizing Lies!	47
Chapter 8: Metamorphosis (Change)!	55
Chapter 9: Spiritual Warfare!	63
Chapter 10: Walking in Victory!	97
Chapter 11: The Greatest of These!	111
Chapter 12: "Psalm 23!"	151
Chapter 13: I "Am"!	159
Chapter 14: His Amazing Resurrection!	177
Conclusion	185

"Only Victory"

No more darkness, only victory you say,
We can have this if only we would faithfully pray.
Pray to You, our Christ and King,
Our Lord and Savior who can do anything.

Why is our faith in You so small,
When You, Oh Lord, are the Savior of all?
We take over so many things in our life,
And groan and complain when we encounter strife.

Help us to seek You first in all we do,
Crushing Satan's lies and holding on to what is true.
No more darkness, only victory You say,
Help us to claim this promise today!

By: Raelene Hudson (2017)

Introduction

John 8:12 (NIV)
*[12] When Jesus spoke again to the people, He said, "**I am the light** of the world. Whoever follows Me will **never** walk in **darkness**, but will have the **light** of life."*

Have you ever been enveloped with such a feeling of darkness that you can barely breathe? It feels like a weight crushing your chest. You try with all your might to step beyond the darkness only to feel the heaviness weighing upon you with each step you try to take.

I have felt this kind of darkness and heaviness in my life. In fact, it became so intense that I began blaming God and asking Him why He would allow me to feel this way? Little did I know how deeply He would go to answer my one word question, "Why?"

I taught eighth grade language arts for thirty-

No More Darkness, Only Victory!

two years and loved what I did. During the last two years of my teaching career, I was helping take care of my parents. My mom had Dementia and my dad Parkinson's. One day when I was leaving for work, my mom asked me why I had to leave? I told her that I had to go to work. On my way to work, I felt the Lord was telling me that I didn't have to go to work but was choosing to go to work. I felt a very clear nudge that He wanted me to refocus my time on my parents instead of on teaching. As a result, I retired from teaching at the end of that school year. I was blessed to spend two incredible years with my mom before she passed away on November 7, 2016. Even though I knew death was part of God's plan, I was heartbroken. I was struggling with the void of losing my mom. Unfortunately, my mom's death was an opportunity Satan began using to keep me emotionally drained.

Three days after burying my mom, my daughter, twenty-four weeks pregnant with her second child, was given a rare and dangerous diagnosis.

Four weeks later on Christmas Eve, my husband had to have emergency surgery for a perforated intestine. Surgery on Christmas Eve and spending Christmas week at the hospital were extra draining since I had not completely recovered from my mom's death or the news of my daughter's high-risk pregnancy.

The next few months were long and exhausting. I was trying to figure out how to live without my mom, my husband couldn't do much physically because of his ileostomy, and I was deeply concerned about my daughter's pregnancy. I knew it was not God's desire for me to spend so much time emotionally drained and walking in a cloud of darkness. I had to take a hard look at where I was focusing my attention, my thoughts, and my energy. I realized without a doubt that I had to make some changes in my life in order to be released from my constant oppression and depression. As I began this painful yet freeing process, I was in awe at what God revealed to me.

At the end of April, during the middle of the night, God woke me up from a deep sleep and prompted me to write a book on being freed from darkness. Within fifteen minutes, He had given me the title and the chapters for this book.

Writing this book has been extremely therapeutic because it has caused me to dig deeply into God's Word and His Truth. Even though I have read these verses before, I am uncovering a deeper understanding because I am asking God to write through me. I don't want these words to just be on paper. It is my desire to bring God the glory He deserves by focusing on His voice, His prompting in my spirit, and His direction.

Through Christ, I believe He desires us to have "***No More Darkness, Only Victory!***"

I am happy to say that my husband has fully recovered, and my daughter gave birth to a healthy beautiful boy.

diagnosis.

Four weeks later on Christmas Eve, my husband had to have emergency surgery for a perforated intestine. Surgery on Christmas Eve and spending Christmas week at the hospital were extra draining since I had not completely recovered from my mom's death or the news of my daughter's high-risk pregnancy.

The next few months were long and exhausting. I was trying to figure out how to live without my mom, my husband couldn't do much physically because of his ileostomy, and I was deeply concerned about my daughter's pregnancy. I knew it was not God's desire for me to spend so much time emotionally drained and walking in a cloud of darkness. I had to take a hard look at where I was focusing my attention, my thoughts, and my energy. I realized without a doubt that I had to make some changes in my life in order to be released from my constant oppression and depression. As I began this painful yet freeing process, I was in awe at what God revealed to me.

At the end of April, during the middle of the night, God woke me up from a deep sleep and prompted me to write a book on being freed from darkness. Within fifteen minutes, He had given me the title and the chapters for this book.

Writing this book has been extremely therapeutic because it has caused me to dig deeply into God's Word and His Truth. Even though I have read these verses before, I am uncovering a deeper understanding because I am asking God to write through me. I don't want these words to just be on paper. It is my desire to bring God the glory He deserves by focusing on His voice, His prompting in my spirit, and His direction.

Through Christ, I believe He desires us to have "**No More Darkness, Only Victory!**"

I am happy to say that my husband has fully recovered, and my daughter gave birth to a healthy beautiful boy.

Reflection

When Jesus promises us in *John 8:12*, we will NEVER walk in darkness, we need to remember that Jesus cannot lie. You may not think this is true, especially when you feel as if your life is in a dark place. Since Jesus is Light and is with us always, we won't ever experience complete darkness. Hold on to the promises in *John 8:12*. Write down your thoughts concerning this verse from our mighty Lord and Savior, Jesus Christ.

Chapter 1
What is Darkness?

Darkness (Noun)
1. Partial or total absence of light
2. Wickedness or evil

Matthew 6:22–23 (NIV)
*²² "The eye is the lamp of the body. If your eyes are healthy, your whole body will be full of light. ²³ But if your eyes are unhealthy, **your whole body will be full of darkness**."*

Since our eyes are the window to our soul, we should keep our eyes on Jesus. What we choose to look at, read, fixate on, etc., determines how the rest of our being becomes. *Matthew 6* spells it out pretty clearly. If our eyes are healthy, we will be full of light. If our eyes are unhealthy, we will be full of darkness.

As Christians we need to have a spiritual eye exam. We need to be honest with ourselves and determine whether we are focusing our sights on Jesus, this world, or any area Satan would tempt us to focus on. We need to ask ourselves if our sights are led by the Holy Spirit or led by Satan? No one else can decide what we choose to focus our attention and thoughts on. Only we, individually, can choose to have healthy eyes.

> *Ephesians 6:12 (KJV)*
> *¹² "For we **wrestle** not against flesh and blood, but against principalities, against powers, against the rulers of the **darkness** of this world, against spiritual wickedness in high places."*

The word wrestle in this verse should set the premise that our lives will contain battles and at times be stressful. When we observe a wrestler, we will notice that they aren't passive in their pursuit of a victory. It is crucial that they determine quickly which moves they must make in order to outsmart their opponent.

Unfortunately, as young or mature Christians,

we are sometimes too passive. If we study our role in our spiritual journey, it is not one that allows us to sit passively and do nothing while expecting God to do all of the work for us. We must realize we are in a spiritual battle every single day where Satan is coming at us with sly and deceptive moves. Sometimes we are blindsided since he is the master of illusion. As a result, we get thrown down.

Darkness is a very real thing. Satan, the Prince of Darkness, is a very real thing. Satan is not going to step away or give us any slack. His goal is to destroy and devour.

1 Peter 5:8 (NKJV)
[8] "Be sober, be vigilant; because your adversary the devil walks about like a roaring lion, seeking whom he may devour."

We need to not tread lightly since Satan truly desires to destroy and devour each and every Christian regardless of age, race, etc. We need to be ready to fight by putting on the Full Armor of

No More Darkness, Only Victory!

God (*Ephesians 6:13-18*).

It is Satan's desire that we hide alone in sin and in darkness. We must come to an understanding that to win our spiritual battle, we must not continue to hide in darkness. Darkness is where Satan wants us to be in order to obliterate us from the face of the earth. We must recognize darkness for what it is, the kingdom where Satan reigns. Satan will always be front and center in the very place where there is spiritual darkness. When we are walking in darkness and Satan has us in his snare, we need to deliberately look into the Word of God to extinguish the darkness and to be flooded with Jesus' Light.

Fortunately, we have the best coach there is, Jesus. When Satan throws us down, we need only to go to our Heavenly Father for help. He is ready to help us at any time and anywhere, but we must obey what He asks us to do: seek Him first, read His Word, trust Him, and go to Him in prayer. With His help, He will tell us how we can outmaneuver Satan in order to get back up. When we are sometimes too passive. If we study our role in our spiritual journey, it is not one that allows us to sit passively and do nothing while expecting God to do all of the work for us. We must realize we are in a spiritual battle every single day where Satan is coming at us with sly and deceptive moves. Sometimes we are blindsided since he is the master of illusion. As a result, we get thrown down.

Darkness is a very real thing. Satan, the Prince of Darkness, is a very real thing. Satan is not going to step away or give us any slack. His goal is to destroy and devour.

1 Peter 5:8 (NKJV)
[8] "Be sober, be vigilant; because your adversary the devil walks about like a roaring lion, seeking whom he may devour."

We need to not tread lightly since Satan truly desires to destroy and devour each and every Christian regardless of age, race, etc. We need to be ready to fight by putting on the Full Armor of

No More Darkness, Only Victory!

God (*Ephesians 6:13-18*).

It is Satan's desire that we hide alone in sin and in darkness. We must come to an understanding that to win our spiritual battle, we must not continue to hide in darkness. Darkness is where Satan wants us to be in order to obliterate us from the face of the earth. We must recognize darkness for what it is, the kingdom where Satan reigns. Satan will always be front and center in the very place where there is spiritual darkness. When we are walking in darkness and Satan has us in his snare, we need to deliberately look into the Word of God to extinguish the darkness and to be flooded with Jesus' Light.

Fortunately, we have the best coach there is, Jesus. When Satan throws us down, we need only to go to our Heavenly Father for help. He is ready to help us at any time and anywhere, but we must obey what He asks us to do: seek Him first, read His Word, trust Him, and go to Him in prayer. With His help, He will tell us how we can outmaneuver Satan in order to get back up. When we are thrown down, we must not admit defeat. With Jesus we are already the victor. We *must claim* "**No More Darkness, Only Victory!**"

When we claim victory and focus on His Light, we will understand that God desires us to know Him on an intimate level in order for His Light to guide us. Satan, however, wants us to remain in darkness so he can blindside us whenever and however he chooses. We need to be ready when Satan tries to throw us down. Instead of letting him pin us down, we need to throw Satan out of the ring for good.

Reflection

What areas of darkness do you need to release to the Lord?

No More Darkness, **Only Victory!**

Is there any area in your life where you are blaming Jesus and not the true enemy, Satan?

Where are you not allowing Jesus' Light to shine causing you to walk in darkness and defeat? Write down these struggles and give them to the Lord, and stop wrestling with Satan over and over. Jesus will free you from this **darkness** when you decide to release it to Him and to walk in His **Light**.

Chapter 2
What is Light?

Light (Noun)
1. The removal of darkness
2. God is light

There is a distinct contrast between darkness and light. Darkness symbolizes evil, while light symbolizes good. God is **light**. He is good.

When I was little, I didn't like the dark. I wanted a night light in my bedroom. Even though the night light only provided a small amount of light, it made me feel less afraid. In this world life can be scary and dark, but Jesus is our night light that never stops shining.

2 Corinthians 4:6 (NKJV)
*⁶ "For it is the God who commanded **light** to shine out of darkness, who has shone in our hearts to give the **light** of the knowledge of the glory of God in the face of Jesus Christ."*

God commanded light to shine out of darkness. That is why He has commanded us to be the light of the world.

Matthew 5:14-16 (NKJV)
*[14] "You are the **light** of the world. A city that is set on a hill cannot be hidden. [15] Nor do they light a lamp and put it under a basket, but on a lamp stand and it gives light to all who are in the house. [16] Let your **light** so shine before men, that they see your good works and glorify your Father in Heaven."*

When in complete darkness, it only takes a small flicker of light to make a difference and to penetrate utter darkness. As Christians, God desires us to be an example allowing our good deeds to glorify Him. He wants us to lead others out of darkness and guide them to Him, the Light of the world. When Satan realizes we are shining brightly for Jesus and guiding the lost to our Savior, he becomes angry and will try to throw us back into darkness over and over again. Satan wants to separate us from the Light that allows us to feel Jesus' presence and love. I praise God that Jesus has given us the following promise:

John 8:12 (NKJV)
*¹² Then Jesus spoke to them again, saying, "I am the **light** of the world. He who follows Me shall **<u>not</u>** walk in darkness, but have the **light** of life."*

This verse is so powerful! Especially if we choose to take this verse apart and apply it in our lives.

1. "JESUS is the **LIGHT** of the world!"

(If any of us have been struggling with anything dark, not from God, we must discover how we can find our way out of this darkness. The only way out is through Jesus Christ, our Savior. We must recognize who Jesus is. He is not our enemy and will never be our enemy. He is the Light! This verse doesn't say He shines a light or is sometimes the light. It clearly says that **He is the Light**. Also, we need to realize He is the Light of the entire world. Darkness will at times seem

No More Darkness, Only Victory!

to encompass not only our lives individually but the entire world. When this happens, we need to realize that our Savior is also the Savior of the world! We need to always focus on the light and not the darkness!)

2. "He who **FOLLOWS** Me!"

(In order to be able to obtain this light, we must follow Jesus. We cannot lead and venture out on our own. We must get into the daily habit of allowing God to lead us and be willing to follow Him. It is so easy to jump ahead of God; therefore, it is important that we see who is in the driver's seat, Jesus or us?)

3. "Shall **not** walk in darkness but have the **LIGHT** of life!"

(If we follow Him, we will NOT walk in darkness and bondage. We will have the constant **Light of Jesus** who is life and freedom. As we follow Him, He will prick our conscience when we are not under His Light or in His will. The verse ends with the promise stating that Jesus' Light is the light of life...not death! Wow! That is a beautiful promise!)

These are incredible promises God gives to us. Jesus is ready to help us anytime and anywhere, but we must obey what He asks us to do. Following Him isn't just about allowing Him to be ahead of us. As we focus on His Light, we must allow Him to lead and to be in control of our lives. We all know the concept of following isn't an easy process to do because most of us like to be in charge of our own lives. My pastor, Larry Petton, always tells us from the pulpit, "God must be president of our lives and not just resident." So true!

Reflection

Where are you not following God? What areas are you leading and not allowing Jesus to be in control of your life? Write these areas down and release them to the Lord. Remember *John 8:12* is a promise that God has given to us, not wishful thinking, but a promise.

Chapter 3
Hearing the Voice of God!

I was once asked if Christians can hear the voice of God? My answer was "yes" since I believe God allows us to hear His voice.

John 10 describes Jesus as being the Good Shepherd who gives His life for His sheep. Jesus states that His sheep **will hear His voice**.

John 10:27 (NKJV)
²⁷ "<u>My sheep hear my voice</u>, and I know them, and they follow Me."

The Holy Spirit comes to live in us when we accept Him as our Savior. Since the Holy Spirit and Jesus are one and the same, His Spirit speaks when we choose to listen to Him.

Over thirty years ago after my two children were born, I began praying every morning that I would be able to hear the voice of God. I prayed this prayer daily for over six months.

During an Easter service, Jesus answered my prayer. As the pastor was concluding his sermon, I felt a prompting in my spirit that I was supposed to stand up and pray for someone's knee. Needless to say, I didn't desire to do this in the least. After all, it was Easter Sunday and more crowded than usual. I didn't want to embarrass myself or the church. I began reasoning with God and telling Him that I didn't think Easter Sunday was an appropriate time since it was so crowded, and I didn't know if it was a man's or woman's knee that I was supposed to pray for. He immediately answered, "Man's." I quickly responded back that I couldn't pray since I didn't know if it was the man's left or right knee. He immediately replied, "Left." I then told Jesus that it would be too humiliating to interrupt what was going on. But as clearly as could be, Jesus reminded me that I had been praying to Him for me to be able to hear His voice. He was now talking to me (His Spirit to my spirit). I knew the choice was up to me if I was going to obey Him. I realized without a doubt that God was truly answering my prayer to be able to hear Him. I knew I had to obey so I timidly stood up and told the pastor that I believed I was supposed to pray for a man's left knee. A man in the back of the church immediately stood up and began to weep. As he walked forward, he told the pastor that he had been praying for several weeks for someone to receive word to pray for his knee because he didn't want to come forward for prayer on his own.

God answered my prayer twofold. First, for the man who was requesting prayer for his knee. Second, that as Christians we can all hear His voice; however, we need to learn to be still and to listen to His voice.

Psalm 46:10 (NIV)
¹⁰ "Be still, and know that I am God..."

I once had a friend ask me to pray for her because she felt I had a direct line to God but that she was on call waiting. At first I thought this was a funny statement but then realized it was rather sad because of what she felt and believed. I realized a lot of Christians believe that God doesn't hear them or answer them. I have learned a valuable truth. None of us are ever on "call waiting." We all have a direct line to God, and His direct line is able to travel in both directions. He tells us in *John 16:13 (NKJV)*:

> *¹³ "However, when He, the Spirit of truth, has come, He will guide you into all truth; for He will not speak on His own authority, but whatever He hears He will speak; and He will tell you things to come."*

I love relationships! I think it is because I believe God created us to have a relationship with Him and with others. Obviously, the more time we spend with others, the more we get to know them. This is the same with our relationship with the Lord. We can't know our Savior the way He desires if we don't spend time with Him in prayer and reading His Word. The more we get to know Jesus, the more we will be able to hear

Him. I honestly don't believe Jesus would die for us and then choose to not talk to us. He desires a relationship with us, but He puts the ball in our court to get to know Him better. He has chosen us, now we must choose Him.

Satan will always try to make us feel unworthy and that we can't possibly hear God. When this happens, we need to remember God's Truth. We can't let Satan take us down the unworthy path. If Jesus died for us, we are worthy! Hallelujah!

Reflection

What is keeping you from hearing God's voice?

No More Darkness, *Only Victory!*

Write down any stronghold, untruth, lack of commitment, or whatever it is that is blocking your relationship with our Savior. He wants to have a direct line of communication with you in order to share His life completely with you.

Chapter 4
Seeking Wisdom!

James 1:5 (NKJV)
*⁵ "If any of you **lacks wisdom**, let him ask of God, who gives to all liberally and without reproach, and it will be given to him."*

The Bible answers almost every question we may have, but we must search for the answers as we seek Him. So many times we Christians choose to walk daily in darkness. It seems easier to walk in the lies of Satan rather than the truths of Jesus. Why is that? We walk around depressed, discouraged, and defeated. We don't press pause and ask ourselves who has placed these negative thoughts, feelings, and lies into our thoughts and actions? Instead we mope around not claiming the victory that is already ours.

2 Timothy 2:26 (NKJV)
²⁶ "...and that they may come to their senses and escape the snare of the devil, having been taken captive by him to do his will."

We have become captive, yet we do not recognize our imprisonment. In order to gain victory in our lives, we must choose to step out of Satan's darkness and into God's Kingdom of Light.

As I have gotten older, I realize more and more that I am sometimes the reason I am in the predicament I am in. Most of the time it is because of my choices. At times, I choose to believe Satan's lies rather than God's promises. I also allow others to plant negative seeds into my thoughts or actions and then ask God to explain why I am suffering consequences. I play the blame game, which causes defeat not victory.

When we read God's Word, He warns us that Satan will constantly try to capture us and imprison us in his lies. I am thankful Jesus tells us what to do in order to escape the snares of the

Devil. At times, it seems we run toward the snare instead of away from it. If we study the following chapter in Proverbs and apply its truth, we will begin to experience freedom from defeat and darkness.

> *Proverbs 2 (NKJV)*
> *1 "My son, if you receive my words, And treasure my commands within you,*
> *2 So that you incline your ear to wisdom, And apply your heart to understanding;*
> *3 Yes, if you cry out for discernment, And lift up your voice for understanding,*
> *4 If you seek her as silver, And search for her as for hidden treasures;*
> *5 Then you will understand the fear of the LORD, And find the knowledge of God.*
> *6 For the LORD gives wisdom; From His mouth come knowledge and understanding;*
> *7 He stores up sound wisdom for the upright; He is a shield to those who walk uprightly;*
> *8 He guards the paths of justice, And preserves the way of His saints.*

No More Darkness, Only Victory!

⁹ Then you will understand righteousness and justice, Equity and every good path.

¹⁰ When wisdom enters your heart, And knowledge is pleasant to your soul,

¹¹ Discretion will preserve you; Understanding will keep you,

¹² To deliver you from the way of evil, From the man who speaks perverse things,

¹³ From those who leave the paths of uprightness To walk in the ways of darkness;

¹⁴ Who rejoice in doing evil, And delight in the perversity of the wicked;

¹⁵ Whose ways are crooked, And who are devious in their paths;

¹⁶ To deliver you from the immoral woman, From the seductress who flatters with her words,

¹⁷ Who forsakes the companion of her youth, And forgets the covenant of her God.

¹⁸ For her house leads down to death, And her paths to the dead;

¹⁹ None who go to her return, Nor do they

regain the paths of life—
*²⁰ So you may walk in the way of goodness,
And keep to the paths of righteousness.*
²¹ For the upright will dwell in the land, And the blameless will remain it;
²² But the wicked will be cut off from the earth, And the unfaithful will be uprooted from it."

When I think of spiritual wisdom, I often think of King Solomon who asked Jesus for wisdom. God answered his request with the following:

2 Chronicles 1:10-12 (NLT)
¹⁰ "Give me the wisdom and knowledge to lead them properly, for who could possibly govern this great people of yours?" ¹¹ God said to Solomon, 'Because your greatest desire is to help your people, and you did not ask for wealth, riches, fame, or even the death of your enemies or a long life, but rather you asked for wisdom and knowledge to properly govern my people— ¹² I will certainly give you the wisdom and knowledge you requested. But I will also give you wealth, riches, and fame such as no

other king has had before you or will ever have in the future!'

We see in this verse how pleased God was with Solomon's request for wisdom and knowledge. Wisdom is defined as the soundness of an action or decision with regard to the application of experience, knowledge, and good judgment. Therefore, spiritual wisdom allows us to use our knowledge of Jesus and His true and inherent Word to make good decisions throughout our lives.

Reflection

Do you ask God daily to provide you with His wisdom? Do you cry out for discernment? If not, why are you waiting?

What area or areas do you need to seek Godly wisdom and discernment? Cry out to Him so He can reveal to you the areas you need to focus on in order to gain wisdom and to see His Light.

Chapter 5
The Word of God!

We live in a society where we are constantly talking, rarely listening with purpose. How many times do we talk to God nonstop asking Him for things, telling Him how and when we would like Him to do things, etc.? When do we truly dig into His Word? When do we pause long enough and sincerely listen to Him? His Word is a complete map for our lives as it tells us which direction to go, which roads to navigate around, which is the best route to take to a destination, etc.

Psalm 119:105 (NKJV)
*105 "Your **Word** is a lamp to my feet and a light to my path."*

Discern what this verse is promising us. His Word is a lamp unto our feet. The Bible, His Word, is a lamp to help guide and direct us through darkness, our fears, our struggles, and our doubts. We must learn to allow His Word to guide each step we take. We also need to allow His Word to guide us <u>before</u> we take a step, not after we take a step.

> *2 Timothy 3:16–17 (NIV)*
> *[16] "All Scripture is God-breathed and is useful for teaching, rebuking, correcting and training in righteousness, [17] so that the servant of God may be thoroughly equipped for every good work."*

It is imperative that we look at what this verse is telling us. ALL scripture, every word from our Savior is God-breathed. Did you catch that? "GOD-BREATHED!" There is no other book, novel, document, etc., that is God-breathed. Nothing! We should run to His Word every time we are needing help of any kind.

He tells us that His Word is useful for teaching. We should be desiring to learn as much as possible about Him, our Lord and Savior. Once we have grasped knowledge from His Word, we are then in a position to share that knowledge with others who come into our lives - our family, our children, the unsaved, those hurting, etc.

He also reminds us that His Word is useful for rebuking, correcting, and training in righteousness. God's Word helps us to correct or straighten up anything that isn't pleasing to Him. When we accept His rebuke or reproof, we begin to notice that our lives will start straightening out. As a result, His righteousness in us will be more transparent to others.

We can be confident that even though everything in this world will die or disappear, God's Word will never go away.

Isaiah 40:8 (NKJV)
[8] "The grass withers, the flower fades, But the Word of our God stands forever."

If we truly believe this to be true, we need to stop investing so much energy and thoughts into temporary help. So many problems happen in our lives and in the world because we do not read God's Word. I have witnessed many Christians who rarely seek God's Word, the Bible; however, they exhaust so much time into self-help books, the internet, counselors, etc. This in and of itself isn't wrong, but it should only be our pursuit <u>after</u> we have searched God's Word for His answer or direction in our lives.

> *Hebrews 4:12 (NKJV)*
> *¹² "For the Word of God is living and powerful, and sharper than any two-edged sword, piercing even to the division of soul and spirit, and of joints and marrow, and is a discerner of the thoughts and intents of the heart."*

One of my favorite parts of this verse is the description of God's Word as being living and powerful. The Word of God is not dead but "living." We can always rely on God's Word because His Word will stand forever and will always be powerful. When are we going to claim this promise and stop allowing Satan to keep us in his web of defeat and deceit? Satan wants us to believe there is no hope and to fall from our faith and our belief in the living God. If the Word is a lamp, then we need to allow His Lamp to shine brightly in our lives.

The Word of God is also "powerful." If we want power in our lives, we need to go to His Word to be filled with His power. When we are exhausted, discouraged, feeling as if we have no hope, etc., we need to open our Bibles and meditate on the promises He gives to us through His Word. We need to place these promises in our hearts and know without a doubt they are from our Heavenly Father. We will never experience all that God desires for us if we don't read and meditate on His Word.

Psalm 86:11 (NKJV)
[11] "Teach me Your way, O Lord: I will walk in Your truth. Unite my heart to fear Your name."

No More Darkness, Only Victory!

Reflection

Have you committed a time each day that you spend reading God's Word? If not, take a moment and think about a time you could schedule to read God's Word. Write this schedule down in the space below and pray for conviction to keep this time with your Heavenly Father. You might even begin a journal on what God is teaching you as you learn to not only read but <u>to study</u> His Word.

Chapter 6
Embracing the Truth!

John 8:32 (NKJV)
*³² "And you shall know the **truth**, and the **truth** shall make you free."*

This verse should have a major impact on our lives since it contains so much power and freedom. I am often surprised at how many of us continually believe in and trust the deceptions from Satan. These deceptions keep us in a continual state of bondage, depression, fear, anger, low self-esteem, doubt, resentment, jealousy, bitterness, and the list goes on.

Jesus tells us that we shall <u>know</u> the **truth**. Before we can walk in truth, we must know what truth is. At the beginning of *John 15*, Jesus declares that He is the real thing, the true vine.

John 15:1 (NIV)
*¹ "I am the **true** vine..."*

There are so many things in today's society that are not true or even real; however, we can confidently place one hundred percent of our trust in Jesus because He promises us He is the true vine. His desire is for us to cling to Him since He will never let us go. We can have confidence that His vine will never break or die. He without a doubt is our Lord, our Father, our Emmanuel, and our true Savior. He is the authentic, true, and everlasting vine that holds everything together. When everything seems to be spiraling out of control, we need only to reach out and cling to Him, the TRUE vine!

He also tells us in...

John 14:6 (NKJV)
⁶ "I am the way, the truth, and the life..."

We continually search for direction and answers to life with no success. Instead we should take God at His Word. God begins the verse describing who He is.

- **HE IS "I AM"!**

    This is His title…"I AM!"

    Exodus 3:14 (NKJV)
    ¹⁴ And God said to Moses, "I AM WHO I AM."

    This title emphasizes the very name of God, Yahweh, which means self-existing or to be. He was! He is! He always will be! Our entire existence and eternal destination hinges on these two words, "I AM". After all, He is the only way to Heaven. We either believe He is the great **I AM** or we don't.

- **HE IS THE WAY!**

    (He is _the way_ to our eternal salvation.)

    John 14:6 (NKJV)
    ⁶ Jesus said to him, "I AM the way, the truth, and the life. No one comes to the Father except through Me."

    (He is _the way_ to meet our needs.)

Philippians 4:19 (NKJV)
¹⁹ "And my God shall supply all your needs according to the riches in glory by Christ Jesus."

(He is _the way_ to direct our paths.)

Proverbs 3:6 (NKJV)
⁶ "In all your ways acknowledge Him, and He shall direct your paths."

(He is _the way_ to bring us peace.)

Ephesians 2:14 (NKJV)
¹⁴ "For He Himself is our peace…"

(He is _the way_ to bring us comfort.)

Psalm 23:4 (NKJV)
⁴ "…For You are with me; Your rod and Your staff, they comfort me."

(He is _the way_ to everything.)

Colossians 1:17 (NKJV)
¹⁷ "And He is before all things, and in Him all things consist."

- **HE IS THE TRUTH!**

Everyone wants proof before they believe something or make a decision about something. As a result, many choose not to believe in Jesus because they cannot find proof He exists. They search and search, ignoring the proof of His existence that is right before their eyes. One very obvious proof is our existence. We are intricately and wonderfully made (*Psalm 139*). Just the way our bodies function with so many intricate and detailed parts can only be the result of a master designer and creator. Our very own life with every breath we take is proof of God's existence. There is no way we are here on this earth and functioning the way our bodies function because of chance or luck. Anyone who chooses not to believe this fact is ignoring what God shows us on a daily basis. Since God cannot lie, everything He tells us is true. God's Word is not just truth, it is the Truth (*Psalm 119:142*).

- **HE IS THE LIFE!**

God created every living creature (*Genesis 1:21*) including human life (*Genesis 2:7*).

John 1:1–5 (NKJV)
*¹ "In the beginning was the Word, and the Word was with God, and the Word was God. ² He was in the beginning with God. ³ All things were made through Him, and without Him nothing was made that was made. ⁴ In Him was **life**, and the **life** was the light of men. ⁵ And the light shines in the darkness, and the darkness did not comprehend it."*

He is in control of life and death for everything and everyone. The only way for any of us to experience eternal life, is to accept Him as our Lord and Savior. *John 3:16* is one of the most widely quoted verses from the Bible.

John 3:16 (NIV)
¹⁶ "For God so loved the world that He gave His one and only Son, that whoever believes in Him shall not perish but have eternal life."

It is my prayer that this verse hasn't become

complacent in our lives since we have probably heard it many times. For Truth (Jesus) to be in our lives and for us to experience eternal life, we must receive Him as our Lord and Savior.

The following is an acronym Jesus gave me on truth...

The
Realization and
Understanding
That
He IS!

It is time we embrace the truth! Jesus is our Lord and Savior!

Reflection

Have you accepted Jesus Christ as your LORD and SAVIOR? If not, pray the following prayer....

Dear Jesus, I know that I am a sinner, and I ask for your forgiveness. I believe You died on the cross for my sins and rose from the dead. I repent from my sins and invite You to come into my heart and life. I desire to trust and follow You as my Lord and Savior! Thank You, Jesus! Amen!

(If you prayed this prayer of salvation, Hallelujah! I want to encourage you to find a Christ-centered church to fellowship in. Share the good news of your salvation with the pastor. Praise the Lord!)

What areas have you been walking in knowing they aren't TRUTHS from God but lies from Satan? Write these lies down (all of them) and determine why you so easily believe these lies. Release these lies to Jesus and then daily focus on His Truths from Scripture so you can experience the freedom Jesus desires you to have.

Chapter 7
Recognizing Lies!

Darkness comes in so many shapes and sizes, but it is most commonly found in lies and deception from Satan. We must never forget that Satan is the FATHER of LIES! He is a master "deceiver!"

When I began praying for this chapter and began to truly pray about Satan being the Father of LIES, God revealed to me that Satan, the Devil, is a Deceiver. I then realized how many areas of our lives the Devil filtrates that all start with the letter D just like his name: "D"EVIL

Death	Darkness	Divorce
Devour	Deceit	Damage
Destroy	Discourage	Disgust
Depression	Deny	Demonic
Doubt	Dissention	Defile
Desolate	Devastation	Deprive

No More Darkness, Only Victory!

Disobedient	Disaster	Dirty
Defeat	Delusion	Devious
Disease	Disloyal	Dishonest
Debt	Doom	Decay
Division	Distorted	Danger
Demolish	Despair	Disgrace

This list could go on and on, but I think you get the idea. The Devil uses any means possible to bring us down, and he will do this time and time again. I have talked to many people who are discouraged about their lives, themselves, others, etc. When I categorize if what they are truly believing is a lie or the truth, it usually falls under the "lie" category.

A lie is defined as a false statement made with deliberate intent to deceive; a falsehood. When we are attacked by lies, it shouldn't surprise us when we discover these lies are strictly coming from Satan since Satan is the father of lies.

John 8:44 (NIV)
⁴⁴ "You belong to your father, the devil, and you

*want to carry out your father's desires. He was a murderer from the beginning, not holding to the truth, for there is no truth in him. When he lies, he speaks his native language, for he is a liar and the **father of lies**."*

In order to recognize a lie, we must learn to decipher when a lie enters our thoughts. We need to study God's Word to begin comprehending what are God's Truths and what are Satan's lies. His lies are deceptive and may at times almost appear to be true. It is important we become sensitive to the prompting of the Holy Spirit to combat Satan's lies when they enter our thoughts since Satan's goal is to destroy and devour.

1 Peter 5:8 (NKJV)
⁸ "Be sober, be vigilant; because your adversary, the devil walks about like a roaring lion, seeking whom he may devour."

Satan often waits until we are physically and emotionally drained to attack. He deceptively allows a lie to appear as the truth which is why we sometimes don't recognize his lie when it penetrates our thoughts. Soon our thoughts cause us to feel helpless and hopeless. When we study God's Word and recognize when deception enters our thoughts, we can take our thoughts captive and release them to the Lord who will cover them with His Truth.

Satan creates a snare for us in order to lure us in and capture us. Satan's first successful snare was with Adam and Eve (*Genesis 3*).

A snare is defined in the Merriam-Webster Dictionary as:

1. something by which one is entangled
2. a position or situation from which it is difficult to escape.

Here are some common snares Satan uses to capture us emotionally, spiritually, and physically:

- rebellion
- pride
- addiction

- lust
- unforgiveness
- jealousy
- anger
- fear
- excessive guilt
- lying spirit
- critical and judging spirit
- greed
- hopelessness
- low self-image
- depression and the other "D" words already mentioned

The list doesn't stop here because we know Satan doesn't stop at anything. In order to truly understand Satan's snares and deception, we must recognize God's Truth which He gives us continually in His Word.

Truth is defined as the facts, the body of real things and events, spiritual reality. The only way to recognize spiritual reality is to know "who" is truth and to know "what" is truth. We also need to believe in truth and to walk in truth. God is Truth!

Satan is the Father of Lies, and Jesus is the Father of Truth. The only way to recognize the difference between the two, is to know who Jesus really is...

> *Ephesians 3:19 (NKJV)*
> *¹⁹ "to <u>know</u> the love of Christ which passes knowledge; that you may be filled with all the fullness of God."*

When we consistently believe in God's Truth, our faith will become stronger and stronger. We will also begin to notice a greater amount of peace and understanding as we quickly discern Satan's distorted lies. When Satan attacks us with these lies, they will ricochet off God's Armor we have surrounding us, heading right back at him. In time, we will begin to experience "**No More Darkness, Only Victory!**"

Reflection

Write down any area you have allowed Satan to deceive you.

Write down areas you know God has revealed truths in your life.

No More Darkness, *Only Victory!*

Do you notice a difference between the two? If so, explain.

Chapter 8
Metamorphosis (Change)!

God has been showing me how our lives are very similar to that of a butterfly. A butterfly goes through several changes or metamorphosis in its lifetime. We, like butterflies, also go through several changes when we become a Christian.

2 Corinthians 5:17 (NKJV)
17 "Therefore, if anyone is in Christ, he is a new creation; old things have passed away; behold, all things have become new."

However, unlike the butterfly, we as Christians don't always change the way Jesus desires or fly free the way He desires us to fly.

The cycle of a butterfly:

- Stage One - The Caterpillar

    The caterpillar is the feeding and growth

stage of the butterfly. It is during this stage that rapid growth takes place causing the caterpillar to shed its skin four or five times as it crawls from place to place. As I was reading about this stage, I was reminded how as new Christians we crawl along at our own pace while at the same time desiring spiritual food and nourishment as our lives around us are constantly changing. These changes cause us to shed our old ways and adapt to the changes God is creating in us and around us. Sometimes these changes aren't easy, and we don't want to shed our skin because we have become comfortable with the skin we are presently in. If we aren't careful, we will continue to crawl with the weight of our lives (sin, etc.) on our back instead of seeking higher ground. Since we have no idea what the next stage of life holds, we need to put our trust in the One who does, our Creator! He is the One who created us and who has created the next stage of our life. It is prideful on our part to not trust in the very One who made us and knows everything about us both now and in our future. God never intended for us to crawl for the rest of our lives. He wants us to grow to the next stage of our lives...the cocoon.

- Stage Two - The Cocoon

The cocoon stage is the stage where transformation takes place. God desires us to be transformed into His image.

2 Corinthians 3:18 (NKJV)
[18] "But we all, with unveiled face, beholding as in a mirror the glory of the Lord, are being transformed in the same image from glory to glory, just as by the Spirit of the Lord."

Unfortunately, we are sometimes allowing Satan to keep us from transforming into what God desires for us. We take our fears, our insecurities, and so much more into our cocoon and wrap the cocoon tightly around ourselves. Sometimes we bring so much garbage into our cocoon, we leave little room for God to make the changes He desires. After a while, we become so comfortable in our cocoon, we want to stay inside and not come out. If only we could see for ourselves that what is on the outside of our cocoon is so much better than what is on the inside. Outside are God's abundant gifts of love and blessings. We will never experience or receive what all God has for us if we are not willing to trust Him and leave the comfort of our cocoon and progress to the next stage...the butterfly.

- Stage Three - Butterfly.

This stage is where mobility takes place. This mobility is the freedom God desires for all of us to experience. We can only experience this freedom when we choose to leave our comfortable cocoon and soar free. In order to experience true freedom and victory, we must leave our past behind - our fears, our insecurities, our lack of faith, and the lies Satan throws at us. We need to spread our wings and trust in our Savior. We must be willing to leave our safety net (cocoon) and be transformed into the incredible butterfly God has created. Once we are soaring and reach higher and higher in our spiritual journey, we will finally see a glimpse of what God has for us... "***No More Darkness, Only Victory!***"

An acronym I created to describe the butterfly:

Believing
Ultimately
That
The
Everlasting
Redeemer
Forever
Loves
You

Once we believe in Him the way He truly desires, we will be able to soar higher and higher as we encompass His love, protection, and freedom in our lives. What better gift can we receive? A gift of freedom soaring with God as He guides us through every storm and every valley. We need to stop crawling on the ground or hiding in our cocoon, and instead choose to soar with Jesus.

No More Darkness, Only Victory!

As we soar, we should:

- Allow the Holy Spirit to guide us.
- See the Lord as the strength in our lives.
- Withstand the storms and learn from them.
- Have strong faith.
- Have courage.
- Be optimistic.
- Develop friendships with people who enrich our lives.
- Express love and care for others.
- Serve God with our spiritual gifts.
- Be quick to forgive and slow to anger.
- Have a servant's heart.
- Impact the lives of others.
- Be fruitful so others will see what we have in Christ.

Reflection

What stage of growth are you in? (Caterpillar, Cocoon, or Butterfly?) Explain why you feel this way.

Are you in the stage God desires you to be? Why or why not?

Chapter 9
Spiritual Warfare!

Warfare...**a battle.** How much do you know about your enemy? God tells us to be prepared to fight Satan daily. The Bible teaches that Satan not only waged war against Jesus, but he also wages war against anyone who follows Jesus. We need to realize how big of a battle we are in. We are in a **spiritual battle** that can happen every single day of our lives.

> *Ephesians 6:12 (NKJV)*
> *12 "For we do not wrestle against flesh and blood, but against principalities, against powers, against the rulers of the darkness of this age, against spiritual hosts of wickedness in the heavenly places."*

Satan is the master of deception. He blends right in and is able to sway our thoughts and actions in such a crafty way that we don't even realize he is there or involved; however, he is there and involved every single time. His deception is so sly and crafty that we aren't aware of it until it is too late.

> *Revelation 12:7–9 (NKJV)*
> *⁷ "And war broke out in heaven: Michael and his angels fought with the dragon; and the dragon and his angels fought, ⁸ but they did not prevail, nor was a place found for them in heaven any longer. ⁹ So the great dragon was cast out, that serpent of old, called the Devil and Satan, <u>who deceives the whole world</u>; he was cast to the earth, and his angels were cast out with him."*

Obviously, this means ALL Christians are in a spiritual battlefield. In any battle, we should be given the proper equipment and training in how to use it. We need to follow God's battle plan on how best to utilize the effective spiritual armor He has provided for us. God's battle plan is for us to put on His Armor daily so that we can be victorious warriors.

THE ARMOR OF GOD

Ephesians 6:10–18 (NKJV)
¹⁰ "Finally, my brethren, be strong in the Lord and in the power of His might. ¹¹ Put on the whole armor of God, that you may be able to stand against the wiles of the devil. ¹² For we do not wrestle against flesh and blood, but against principalities, against powers, against the rulers of the darkness of this age, against spiritual hosts of wickedness in the heavenly places. ¹³ Therefore take up the whole armor of God, that you may be able to withstand in the evil day, and having done all, to stand. ¹⁴ Stand therefore, having girded your waist with truth, having put on the breastplate of righteousness, ¹⁵ and having shod your feet with the preparation of the gospel of peace; ¹⁶ above all, taking the shield of faith with which you will be able to quench all the fiery darts of the wicked one. ¹⁷ And take the helmet of salvation, and the sword of the Spirit, which is the word of God; ¹⁸ praying always with all

prayer and supplication in the Spirit, being watchful to this end with all perseverance and supplication for all the saints—"

God's Armor brings victory because it is more than a protective covering. It is the very life of Christ Himself.

Romans 13:12–14 (NIV)
[12] "The night is nearly over; the day is almost here. So let us put aside the deeds of darkness and put on the armor of light. [13] Let us behave decently, as in the daytime, not in carousing and drunkenness, not in sexual immorality and debauchery, not in dissension and jealousy. [14] Rather, **clothe yourselves with the Lord Jesus Christ***, and do not think about how to gratify the desires of the flesh."*

When we put on "His" Armor, not someone else's armor but HIS Armor, He surrounds us and keeps us safe. Notice we are clothing ourselves with Jesus Himself. It is HIS Armor we are putting on! Isn't that incredible? We are wrapping ourselves with the Lord Jesus Christ! Praise Him always!

In order to be victorious we must be prepared to "stand" against evil. This means we are not to retreat or to give up. We can only remain standing if we unite with God and use His Armor. God's Armor is compared to the armor that Roman soldiers wore to protect themselves in physical battle. Since our battles are mostly spiritual battles, God has given us His Spiritual Armor to protect us **if** and **when** we put it on. He is always ready to help us be victorious in battle, but we must do our part by praying and clothing ourselves with His entire Armor. We need to get into the habit of putting on His Armor every day since Satan will come at us daily.

It is important that we dissect this armor so we know the importance of each piece.

- **The Belt of Truth**

    Ephesians 6:14a (NKJV)
    14 "Stand therefore, having girded your waist

with truth..."

Truth is absolute. It is not what we see, feel, hear, etc. It must reflect back to HIS Truth or it isn't truth.

A belt was the first piece of armor to be put on by the soldiers because it held their scabbard and sword in place.

Spiritually, truth should be the first piece we as Christians put on. We need to cinch or tighten the belt of truth (Jesus) which holds the sword (His Word) in place. When we tighten truth around us and allow this truth to carry His Word, we will begin to experience freedom. Truth sets us free while sin weighs us down.

Hebrews 12:1b (NKJV)
1b "...let us lay aside every weight, and the sin which so easily ensnares us, and let us run with endurance the race that is set before us..."

John 8:32 (NKJV)
32 "And you shall know the truth, and the truth

shall make you free."

If we don't tighten our belt, we are constantly having to readjust what is falling down around us. God doesn't want us to continually readjust our lives. Instead, He wants us to tighten our belt of truth and walk steadily allowing His Truth to guide our steps.

God doesn't just desire us to know His Truth, but to envelop ourselves in His Truth. God's revelation (His Truth) is made up of all that He **is** to us, and all that He **has done** for us, and all that He **promises** to do for us in the days ahead. This is the wonderful and everlasting truth that is written in His Word and revealed by Jesus Christ and the Holy Spirit. This truth protects us from the lies of this world and from Satan.

Reflection

Jesus is Truth! We must walk in Truth (Jesus) and believe in Truth (Jesus) in order to be free from the "bondage" of Satan. Take a moment and write down any area you are not walking in truth but

No More Darkness, *Only Victory!*

instead are walking in the weight of sin or lies.

What areas keep falling down around you because you do not have His Truth tightened around your waist?

- **Breastplate of Righteousness**

Ephesians 6:14b (NKJV)
*14b "...having put on the breastplate of **righteousness**..."*

We are to put on the breastplate of righteousness. The soldiers' breastplate protected their vital organs from the onslaught of the enemy, especially when the enemy attacked from unexpected directions.

As Christians, we need to protect our heart and other vital areas from Satan's attacks because he comes at us from all directions. In order for the breastplate to be beneficial, it must be made of righteousness (God's standards of righteous living).

The definition of righteousness is free from guilt or sin. I believe part of the reason we walk in darkness and do not walk in victory against Satan is because we constantly walk in sin without taking our spiritual temperature. If we are not living a righteous life, we open ourselves to more attacks from Satan. I love this quote: "Sin will keep us from the Bible, or the Bible will keep us from sin."

Are we on fire for the Lord or for ourselves? How do we treat those closest to us? How do we treat others in general? Where is most of our energy going...serving or seeking self?

> *1 John 3:7–8 (NKJV)*
> *⁷ "Little children, let no one deceive you. He who practices righteousness is righteous, just as He is righteous. ⁸ He who sins is of the devil, for the devil has sinned from the beginning. For this purpose the Son of God was manifested, that He might destroy the works of the devil."*

Reflection

Our spiritual heart determines our actions, etc. God's breastplate protects our heart. What areas do you need to give to the Lord that are keeping you from living in righteousness? Dig deep...

- **The Footwear**

Ephesians 6:15 (NKJV)
*[15] "and having shod (fitted) your feet with the preparation of the gospel of **peace**..."*

At first, we may not think of our feet as being very important in the armor of protection. However, when reading this verse, we need to look at the word "preparation." A victorious soldier had to be prepared for battle. A Roman's battle shoes were studded with spikes to help him stay upright in different types of terrain. If the soldier fell down, the enemy had a better chance to overtake him. Satan is waiting for us to fall down so he can pounce on us and capture us. We need to prepare for our spiritual battle <u>before</u> we walk into the unknown, <u>not after</u>.

Even though the studded spikes were important to stay upright, God's peace is also of utmost importance. God gives us the freedom to choose what we do and where we walk. At times we choose to not go where God desires us to go or go into areas that are not pleasing to Him. As a result, we are not in His will and experience turmoil in our hearts instead of experiencing peace. The Hebrew word for peace is shalom (completeness, success, fulfillment, wholeness, harmony, security, and well being).

God knew we would need His peace in our lives. He desires us to walk in His peace. Peace has to be internal before it can be external. Once we experience internal peace, we are prepared to spread the gospel of God's salvation and peace with others. This is what the gospel of peace is all about. When we are spiritually at peace, we can be strong in the face of a spiritual battle. When we are prepared in this way, we are able to <u>stand firm</u> and not fall down.

I love the way *Romans 10:15* states this concept.

> *Romans 10:15 (NKJV)*
> *[15] "And how shall they preach unless they are sent? As it is written: "How beautiful are the feet of those who preach the gospel of peace, Who bring glad tidings of good things!"*

This verse is a reminder to us that we are to preach the gospel of the good news...the news of salvation which brings peace to those who trust God as their Lord and Savior.

My acronym for PEACE:
- **P**raying
- **E**very day
- **A**cknowledging
- **C**hrist's
- **E**verlasting love

No More Darkness, Only Victory!

Reflection

How are you preparing to "stand firm" against Satan?

What areas cause you to stumble and fall, making you an easy target for Satan?

What areas are you not walking in peace? Explain how this may be keeping you from experiencing the peace God desires you to have in your life.

Look up the following verses and write them down to help you walk in peace.

Ephesians 2:14; Philippians 4:7; Colossians 3:15; Romans 15:13; Jeremiah 29:11; John 14:27

- **The Shield of Faith**

    Ephesians 6:16 (NKJV)
    16 "above all, taking the shield of faith with which you will be able to quench <u>all</u> the fiery darts of the wicked one."

A shield was vitally important to a soldier because it provided a blanket of protection. It was the first barrier of defense against the attacks of the enemy.

This is one of my favorite parts of God's Armor. Why? Because of several important factors. First, this verse starts out with "above all." There are several synonyms for above all: most of all, chiefly, mainly, especially, and essentially. It is obvious the shield is a very important piece of God's Armor, if not the most important.

Second, look at the promise of what the shield of faith does. When we put on the shield of faith, it **will quench (stop) all** of the fiery darts of Satan. There are three key words in this verse we need to focus on. These words are dynamic because of their strength.

Will is not "maybe." There are many things in this life that encompass the concept of maybe, but we can be sure that God's shield of faith is not one of them. Jesus' shield of faith WILL defeat Satan.

Stop is "definite." Stop means to come to an end. We can rest assured knowing Jesus' shield will put an end to the fiery darts of Satan.

All is not "some." When we cover ourselves with His shield (Jesus), not one of Satan's darts will penetrate our lives.

Our shield of faith can only be as strong as we choose to make it. Its strength will be determined by how much we believe in God and by how much we trust Him.

Another part of our shield is how each shield can be joined together. God does not want us to be alone in our battles but to be united with other believers. As a body of believers, we can join with other believers and put our shields together. This can allow us to become a stronger force against Satan's fiery darts when he fires them at our children, our relationships, our marriage, our health, etc. I can envision these darts ricocheting off each shield and heading straight back to stab and defeat Satan. That is victory!

Finally, putting on this piece of armor is important because we need to believe in its true purpose, which is learning to engage our faith in Christ.

James 2:20 (NKJV)
[20] "But do you want to know, O foolish man, that faith without works is dead?"

Reflection

Where is your faith and trust in Jesus?

Raelene Hudson

How strong is your shield? (Explain)

What areas are you not trusting His ability to do what He promises?

- **The Helmet of Salvation**

    Ephesians 6:17a (NKJV)
    *17a "And take the helmet of **salvation**…"*

    A soldier's helmet protected his head and his brain. What does the helmet of salvation actually mean? Salvation is who we are in Christ! We are His for eternity!

    Our spiritual helmet protects our minds from the lies Satan tries to put into our thoughts. Satan is constantly after our minds. We must continually remember that so many of our spiritual battles start with our thoughts. Don't let Satan entangle your thoughts! Remember who you are in Christ!

    When we receive Christ as our Lord and Savior, we are saved. Satan does not want us to rest in our salvation. He wants us to constantly be discouraged or question our security in Christ. When we are discouraged, we can lose our hope and our joy. Jesus desires for us to have hope and joy in our daily lives and to remember we are identified with Christ and in Christ because of our salvation.

1 Thessalonians 5:8–9 (NKJV)
⁸ "But let us who are of the day be sober, putting on the breastplate of faith and love, and as a helmet the hope of salvation. ⁹ For God did not appoint us to wrath, but to obtain salvation through our Lord Jesus Christ..."

Hebrews 6:19a (NIV)
¹⁹ᵃ "We have this hope as an anchor for the soul, firm and secure..."

He knew we would need to be anchored and secure in Him. The helmet also protects the Christian's eyes because Jesus wants us to keep our sights continually on Him.

Hebrews 12:1–2 (NKJV)
*¹ "Therefore we also, since we are surrounded by so great a cloud of witnesses, let us lay aside every weight, and the sin which so easily ensnares us, and let us run with endurance the race that is set before us, ² **looking** unto Jesus, the author and finisher of our faith, who for*

the joy that was set before Him endured the cross, despising the shame, and has sat down at the right hand of the throne of God."

This joy and hope can be ours if and when we daily place the helmet of salvation upon our heads. By doing this, we are always reminded of our salvation and what Christ did for us on the cross.

Nehemiah 8:10 (NKJV)
[10] "do not sorrow, for the joy of the Lord is your strength."

Jesus did the one thing that should prove His unconditional love for us...He died for us! What more could He have done to demonstrate His love for us? Comprehending this truth should bring us joy in Who we serve and provide strength to help us in our spiritual battles.

Reflection

If you struggle with your security in Christ or the lies which Satan constantly throws your way on a continual basis, write these struggles and lies down and pray daily for God's helmet of protection.

No More Darkness, Only Victory!

Become secure in your salvation with Christ by going to His Word and write down as many verses as you can find that show you exactly who we are in Christ.

Example:

"I am a child of God." (John 1:12)
"I am reconciled to God." (Romans 5:11)
"I am a temple in which God dwells." (1 Corinthians 3:16)
"I am a citizen of Heaven." (Philippians 3:20)

Continue adding to these incredible promises God has given to us, His children.

- **The Sword of the Spirit**

    Ephesians 6:17b (NKJV)
    *17b "And take the helmet of salvation, and the **sword** of the Spirit, which is the Word of God."*

A soldier's sword was used to penetrate the enemy. God's Word is described as a sword because it is God's desire for His Word to penetrate our hearts and thoughts. His Word needs to penetrate the lies the enemy entangles us with on a daily basis.

Hebrews 4:12 (NKJV)
12 "For the word of God is living and powerful, and sharper than any two-edged sword, piercing even to the division of soul and spirit, and of joints and marrow, and is a discerner of the thoughts and intents of the heart."

I love how Hebrews describes the sword (His Word) as being living and powerful. It is important that we notice the two adjectives describing His Word...LIVING and POWERFUL! The only way we can use His Word to battle for us, is IF we truly believe in its power and that it is not dead but is as much alive now as it was in Biblical times. Plus, we need to believe that it is sharper than any two-edged sword. Are we keeping our swords sharp by reading and believing that His word is alive and powerful? When we realize the sword is His Spirit, His living and powerful Word, we can move forward to attack the enemy in close combat.

The sword of the Spirit is the only weapon of God's Armor. The rest of His Armor is our protective gear to protect us from the enemy. The Sword (His Word) is the weapon we can victoriously use against Satan. The root word of sword is WORD. I don't believe it is a coincidence that His SPIRIT surrounds the WORD allowing it to become the S-**WORD** of the SPIRIT.

I have kept a lot of letters from friends and family because I love to go back and reread them from time to time. God literally gave us His tangible Word to read and reread over and over again. Jesus wants us to hide His Word in our hearts (*Psalm 119:11*) in order for us to use it in our spiritual battles. To be successful in battle, we must constantly keep our swords sharp by studying the Word of God.

Reflection

Have you allowed your sword to become dull? If so, what can you do to begin the process of sharpening each side of your sword?

Write down some of your favorite verses that have ministered to you.

- **Prayer**

    Ephesians 6:18 (NKJV)
    *18 "**Praying** always with all prayer and supplication in the Spirit, being watchful to this end with all perseverance and supplication for all the saints—"*

    Prayer is how we communicate with our Lord and Savior. When studying and learning about prayer, God gave me this acronym:

Purposeful
Relationship
Asking
You, Our Lord,
Earnestly for Your
Revelation in our lives!

Philippians 4:6 (NKJV)
⁶ "Be anxious for nothing, but in everything by prayer and supplication, with thanksgiving, let your requests be made known to God."

We are to pray fervently for ourselves, the church, and others. Prayer is our direct line to God and reminds us Who should be in charge of our lives. Prayer and His Word are the best defense in our spiritual battle.

Another powerful verse on prayer that should bring us confidence when we pray is

1 John 5:14-15 (NKJV)
¹⁴ "Now this is the confidence that we have in Him, that if we ask anything according to His will, He hears us. ¹⁵ And if we know that He

hears us, whatever we ask, we know that we have the petitions that we have asked of Him."

I believe many Christians don't interpret this verse the way God intended.

Jesus wants us to have confidence in our prayers to Him. He wants us to remember who HE is and to come into His presence when we pray. He wants us to remember that He will never leave us but is always with us.

An important part of this verse we shouldn't omit is "according to His will." We can ask anything IF it is according to His will and can rest assured that He hears us. Sometimes I think we go to Him asking Him for things that He does not desire or will for us or for our loved ones. God answers every prayer and hears every prayer we send to Him. We know that His answer may at times be "Yes" or "No" or "Not Now!" Since He is perfect, we should believe without a doubt that His answer is the "perfect" answer for us even if we don't understand why He answers some of our prayers the way He does.

We all know trusting His answers isn't always easy to do, but it is what Jesus has asked us to do as we draw closer to Him. We need to always remember how much He loves us and wants only the best for us. Because He is all-knowing, we can have confidence that when we pray to Him, He will answer our particular prayer with His perfect will allowing us to receive the victory He desires for us to experience!

We now have the full armor God has provided at our fingertips. We need to put HIS Armor on daily and not just when it is convenient. When we choose to put on God's entire Armor, we will be prepared to fight Satan and his schemes of deceit, defeat, discouragement, pride, low self-esteem, depression, neglect, rejection, etc. And remember whatever battle we face, Jesus promises us that we will never have to fight alone! He is always with us. (*Matthew 28:20; Hebrews 13:5*)

Praise Him Always!!

Reflection

What piece of armor is your weakest? Explain why?

What areas do you need to change in your life concerning your thoughts and actions in order to place God's entire Armor of protection on you and your family each and every day?

What is your prayer life like? Write down your thoughts on prayer. Reflect on ways to improve your prayer life.

Chapter 10
Walking in Victory!

3 John 4 (NIV)
⁴ "I have no greater joy than to hear that My children are walking in the truth."

I believe our freedom from darkness is correlated with our walk with our Lord and Savior. Are we completely dedicated to God, or only halfway? Most of the time we get out of life whatever we put into it. This is a pretty simple concept but one we disregard because of its simplicity. God did not make our Christian walk to be extremely difficult. He tells us everything we need to know to have victory. He gives us freedom to choose what we do everyday. As a result, we must realize that our choices have consequences. God knew we would have trouble every day with Satan and with the turmoil that plagues us almost every single day. This is why He tells us to seek Him first...each and every day!

As a school teacher, I love tangible items when teaching and always think of the cross when I think of Jesus. Not just because He hung on a cross but because of what the cross represents. As Jesus died and hung on the cross, it is important that we, as His children, realize His posture on the cross. His body hung in the shape of the cross as a physical reminder of the importance He placed on our relationship with Him and with others. The cross is vertical and horizontal.

We must first build our relationship with God!

Matthew 6:33 (KJV)
*33 "But seek ye **first** the kingdom of God..."*

By seeking God first, we have a vertical relationship with Him. Early in my Christian walk, I used to go to other people for advice and read whatever books I could get my hands on to try and rescue myself out of a trying situation. This wasn't wrong in God's eyes, but it was in the wrong order. God desires us to seek Him first instead of last.

When we have a relationship with Christ, we are then able to have a relationship with others which is the horizontal relationship of the cross. *Ecclesiastes* 4 says it so well:

> *Ecclesiastes 4:9–12 (NKJV)*
> *⁹ "Two are better than one, Because they have a good reward for their labor. ¹⁰ For if they fall, one will lift up his companion. But woe to him who is alone when he falls, For he has no one to help him up. ¹¹ Again, if two lie down together, they will keep warm; But how can one be warm alone? ¹² Though one may be overpowered by another, two can withstand him. And a threefold cord is not quickly broken."*

I find it so bizarre that when we are struggling physically, we can so easily share our physical struggles with each other and seek medical help and advice. But when we are struggling spiritually, we pretend all is good and do not share what is happening in our spiritual lives. Satan's goal is for us to be alone so he can more easily attack us and cause us to fall. Jesus' goal is for us to stand firm and to have a relationship with Him and with each other so we can love Him and others the way He desires.

When we study *John 15:1-8*, we can learn even more about seeking God first and our relationship with Him.

John 15:1-8 (NKJV)
[1] "I am the true vine, and My Father is the vinedresser. [2] Every branch in Me that does not bear fruit He takes away; and every branch that bears fruit He prunes, that it may bear more fruit. [3] You are already clean because of the word which I have spoken to you. [4] Abide in Me, and I in you. As the branch cannot bear fruit of itself, unless it abides in the vine, neither can you, unless you abide in Me. [5] I am the vine, you are the branches. He who abides in Me, and I in him, bears much

fruit; for without Me you can do nothing. ⁶ If anyone does not abide in Me, he is cast out as a branch and is withered; and they gather them and throw them into the fire, and they are burned. ⁷ If you abide in Me, and My words abide in you, you will ask what you desire, and it shall be done for you. ⁸ By this My Father is glorified, that you bear much fruit; so you will be My disciples."

These verses are about Jesus being the vine and we being the branches. At the very beginning of *John 15*, Jesus declares that He is the real thing - the true vine.

John 15:1 (NKJV)
¹ "I am the true vine, and My Father is the vinedresser."

He isn't an imposter but rather is our Lord and Savior. <u>He is the only one who can sustain us</u>. As we mature in Christ, it is imperative that we understand without any doubt who Jesus truly is. He is the Beginning and the End, the First and the Last, the Alpha and the Omega, the Messiah, the Chief Corner-Stone, the Everlasting God, the Lord of Lords, and the King of Kings. Obviously, Jesus is the divine source of an abundant spiritual harvest.

The Vinedresser is the one who takes care of the entire vineyard. It is His responsibility to nurture, trim, and take care of the vine. He takes a deep interest in the vine's growth and productivity. God appointed His Son, Jesus, to be the TRUE vine. We become the branches when we by faith accept Him as our Lord and Savior. I praise God that we are the ones chosen to be His branches!

Our entire existence is about relationships with Jesus and with each other.

John 15:2–4 (NKJV)
² "Every branch in Me that does not bear fruit He takes away; and every branch that bears fruit He prunes, that it may bear more fruit.
³ You are already clean because of the Word

which I have spoken to you. ⁴ *Abide in Me, and I in you. As the branch cannot bear fruit of itself, unless it abides in the vine, neither can you,* ***unless you abide in Me.***"

We cannot bear fruit without abiding in Him.

I believe that as Christians, we don't always think about the consequences of our actions. Our fruit should resemble the vine (Jesus) that we (the branches) are connected to. When we abide in Him and allow the Vinedresser (God) to tend to everything, then we will be aware that Jesus did not create us to be independent of Him but <u>to be dependent on Him</u>. I love the first eight words at the beginning of this verse:

John 15:5a (NKJV)
^{5a} "I am the vine, you are the branches..."

Jesus is the vine and we are the branches. Pause for a moment and dwell on this reality. We are <u>attached</u> to the "true" vine. We are attached in order to be continually nourished and fed. The vine (Jesus) is the source which produces everything necessary for us to live, to grow, to mature, and to become what God created us to be.

Jesus clearly tells us our role and place in His divine order. Jesus allows us and desires for us to be His branches. Nothing is as closely attached or connected to the vine than the branches. Without Jesus we would not have life. We are truly blessed to be His!

> *John 15:5 (NKJV)*
> *5b "He who abides in Me, and I in him, bears much fruit; <u>for without Me you can do nothing</u>."*

Separation is such a lonely and scary place. While this is a normal process of growing up, it can be a stumbling block in our spiritual lives. Especially when we choose to separate from God and His Word. Yet, that is what we so often do. We become prideful as we continue our journey in this life without remaining in Jesus. At some point, we edge God out (EGO) and try to do things on our own, apart from Him. Do we truly believe we can do things better than the Creator Himself? He specifically tells us in

John 15:5 (NKJV)
⁵ "for without Me you can do nothing!"

Another realization about the grapevine is the grapes are clustered together. This is how Jesus wants us to be as a Christian family... clustered together. Our entire existence is about relationships with each other and with Jesus.

Another acronym from the Lord:

> **A**lways
> **B**eing
> **I**n His
> **D**ivine
> **E**xcellence

We can walk in **victory** by seeking Him <u>first</u> and <u>abiding</u> in Him every single day!

We also need to remember that like the grapevines, we need water to sustain us. Jesus Christ is our living water who sustains us each and every day. I have written a poem about Jesus being our living water.

"Jesus, the Living Water"

You are the Living Water who allows me to never thirst again,
You are the Living Water who cleanses me of all my sin.
You are the Living Water flowing through my spirit and my veins,
With me always through the pounding storms and the gentle rains.

As the deer panteth for water, so my soul longeth after thee,
You alone can quench my thirst and set my spirit free.
I will satisfy my spiritual thirst with Your Living Water each and every day,
As You comfort me, protect me, and guide me along the way.

I will share Your Living Water with others as it overflows from me,

Raelene Hudson

Sharing Your Living Water so that others can live for eternity.
Your Living Water is a gift that You paid the price to give,
Dying on the cross so that for eternity I could live.

You offer Your Water of eternal life to everyone on this earth,
Hoping they will realize their value and their worth.
Let us empty ourselves daily and allow You to fill our cup,
Keeping our spirits from falling and always being lifted up!

No More Darkness, Only Victory!

Reflection

Do you feel connected or disconnected from God? Explain...

What is keeping you from walking with Jesus, our Savior, our true vine?

If you are struggling with feeling like you are not connected to the vine (Jesus), ask Jesus to reveal to you any areas you are giving to Satan, and then give those areas to the Lord, our Living Water.

Chapter 11
The Greatest of These!

Have you ever wondered why there is so much pain in the world? Why do so many Christians not have any hope or joy? Why do so many seem to have trouble loving themselves or others? Why is it especially hard for us as Christians to have faith in Jesus?

For many years, I continually asked why and began trying to figure out how to fix the pain and hurt that I noticed around me. Okay, a rather large task, but I felt I had to begin somewhere. It wasn't long into my journey that God spoke directly to my heart and told me that each of us needed to fix ourselves before we try to fix anything or anyone else. What a dose of truth serum! Therefore, I began doing that - looking inward instead of outward. What a difference that has made! That was over 20 years ago, and I am still looking inward because I have discovered that our walk as Christians is a journey that will take us down many roads. Roads that are sometimes smooth and sometimes bumpy. But with God as the driver, we never have to worry about where the road goes or ends up. We just need to be willing to allow God to take us wherever He desires. When we grasp this truth, we can begin looking outward knowing that He will send others across our paths to share the love of Christ.

Life is complicated. The world isn't perfect. But for the most part, life can be centered around *1 Corinthians 13*.

> *1 Corinthians 13:13 (NLT)*
> *¹³ "Three things will last forever—**faith, hope, and love**—and the greatest of these is love."*

It has been my desire to study these three areas to see why God would tell us that these three areas would endure when everything else may not in this imperfect, complicated world. I also wanted to see how I measured up in these three areas of faith, hope, and love. It didn't take me long to realize I had allowed these three areas to become somewhat complacent instead of a dynamic force in my life.

In order to become better or make progress, we must look intently and truthfully into our own lives to see where we truly are in our spiritual journey. When I started doing this, I began to see why God wanted to turn most of my focus inward instead of outward.

In my twenties, much of my life was lived in ignorance. I didn't really know my Heavenly Father the way He wanted me to know Him. I discovered it was hard to understand and absorb something I didn't know much about. I thought I knew Him, but I didn't know Him well enough to have the type of faith, hope, and love He desired me to have.

As time evolved, I discovered that God is Omniscient (all-knowing), Omnipresent (everywhere), and Omnipotent (all powerful).

Once I grasped these three areas and fully understood them, I began to realize just how sovereign God is. Because He is all-knowing, everywhere at all times, and all-powerful, nothing catches Him by surprise. He will accomplish His plan as well as keeping His promises! Letting go and letting God really does result in **"No More Darkness, Only Victory!"**

I have also discovered that Christianity isn't a quick fix but a lifetime process. A lifetime of being willing to learn, to change, and to grow in the way God desires.

Since the three areas of faith, hope, and love are so important; we should be willing to learn as much about them as possible and then apply them into our lives so we can experience an enduring life of spiritual victory instead of spiritual defeat.

I used to ask God why He allowed so much despair in the world? We sometimes become despaired because of our lack of faith, our lack of hope, and our lack of love. I discovered that these three areas encompass almost every area as they are intertwined into our personal lives.

God revealed a lot to me as I spent time in prayer seeking His will and His direction in the areas of faith, hope, and love. With this knowledge and understanding, I experienced a freedom which allowed me to be more of what Christ desired me to be. It is my desire to be a person of **faith** who experiences **hope** while receiving and giving **love** as God desires.

AREA ONE: FAITH

Hebrews 11 defines faith in the following way:

Hebrews 11:1 (ESV)
*1 "Now **faith** is the assurance of things hoped for, the conviction of things not seen."*

Hebrews 11 has the word FAITH written twenty-seven times! Obviously, faith is something God thinks is important.

Webster's definition of faith is reliance, loyalty, or complete trust in God.

I had to ask myself where I stood in the area of faith? Did I truly rely on God? Was I completely loyal to God? Did I completely trust in God?

Even though I was a Christian, the answer was no. Therefore, I had to figure out why? Why was it so hard to rely on God and to trust Him with everything in my life? I knew part of the answer was fear. I was afraid of letting go and letting God have my entire life. I was afraid to take the necessary step of blind faith. I wanted to know the beginning, the middle, and the end before I gave it to God. Pathetic I know, but true! I soon discovered I was not alone in this area. Most of us are afraid to rely on God and to completely trust Him. We say we trust Him in our minds and hearts, but our actions speak differently.

Hebrews 11:6a (NLT)
*6a "And it is impossible to please God without **faith**..."*

What a clear and direct statement! It is impossible to please God without faith. As

Christians, we should desire daily to please God. We need to learn to have faith in Him in order to believe in "who" He is and to believe in "what" He says. We should stand firm in the One who was, who is, and who is to come. (*Revelation 1:8*) It seems easier to follow our will or to follow Satan's lies than it does to follow the promises of God. Why is it so hard for us to believe in the One who can never lie? Are we too afraid to allow this concept of truth to be what transpires in our lives? Possibly, since we are a country wrought in despair, depression, unhappiness, and misery as we fall to our knees out of exhaustion and weakness. Instead, we should be soaring with wings of an eagle as we experience the joy of our Lord who renews our strength.

Isaiah 40:31 (NKJV)
³¹ "But those who wait upon the Lord shall renew their strength; They shall mount up with wings like eagles. They shall run and not be weary, they shall walk and not faint."

Unfortunately, we complain about so many

things and find ourselves at times blaming God for certain situations, when we ourselves are the very ones who may have caused the situation in the first place. We say we have faith but then wonder if God is really going to do what He promises.

During my quiet time with the Lord one morning, He revealed to me that my faith in Him was limited. I didn't always trust Him to do what He promised. I put Him in a box and tried to take over certain things that I thought I could somehow do better than He could do.

I had to learn that in order for Him to do anything in my life, I had to truly believe that He was a BIG enough God who could do anything. As a result, He gave me an acronym that has helped me to refocus my thinking.

> **B**elieve
> **I**n
> **G**od

I asked Him to allow me to understand the exact meaning behind this acronym.

1. We **don't believe** in Him because we **doubt** Him.

2. We **doubt** Him because we **don't trust** Him.

3. We **don't trust** Him because we choose to **take over** certain things.

4. We **take over** because we don't really think He will do what we **desire**.

5. We **desire** things that may not be what is **best** for us.

6. When the **best** does not result in what we expected, we are upset with Him for giving us what we **wanted**.

This acronym is simple. God is a **BIG** God who can do anything.

I began realizing my shield of faith was only as strong as my faith in Him. I could not stop the fiery darts of Satan, if my faith wasn't one hundred percent placed in Jesus, my Savior! What should faith look like in a Christian's life? It should begin with our reliance on God - our complete trust in Him. I realized I didn't truly rely on God or trust Him the way He desired. I relied on myself or others much quicker than I did on Him. Rather naive on my part when I take into account *Mark 10:27*.

> *Mark 10:27 (NKJV)*
> *²⁷ "But Jesus looked at them and said, "With men it is impossible, but not with God; for with God **all** things are possible."*

Why did I rely on myself more than I did on God? His Word promises that nothing is impossible with Him. Since I didn't have an answer, I had to refocus my thoughts and actions. I had to begin relying on God and His promises. I had to start putting my confidence and trust completely in Him. After all, He is the One Who created me and Who knows me better than anyone else. He is also the One Who can see the future and knows my every thought. *Psalm 139* states it so clearly:

Psalm 139:1–6 (NLT)
¹ "O LORD, you have examined my heart and know everything about me. ² You know when I sit down or stand up. You know my thoughts even when I'm far away. ³ You see me when I travel and when I rest at home. You know everything I do. ⁴ You know what I am going to say even before I say it, LORD. ⁵ You go before me and follow me. You place your hand of blessing on my head. ⁶ Such knowledge is too wonderful for me, too great for me to understand!"

Wow! These verses should make us happy as we soak in the knowledge that God is not against us but for us! We can rest in the assurance that God can do a much better job with our lives than we can.

The entire process of putting my faith in God did not happen overnight. Each situation that occured in my life, required me to step back and decide where I was going to place my faith and trust. As time progressed, I began to rely and depend more and more on God and less on myself. I began to truly let go and let God have me, my family, my life - all of it. What a freeing experience it has become! Do I lapse back from time to time and try to hang on to certain things? Yes! But God always pricks my conscience in order for me to let go of my death grip and allow Him to guide me through whatever journey I am on.

I am often reminded of the verse:

Isaiah 7:9 (NIV)
*⁹ "If you do not stand firm in your **faith**, you will not stand at all."*

How can I argue with that? If I am not standing firm in putting my faith in Jesus, I will not be standing but falling into whatever pit is opening its ugly gate to swallow me up.

Ephesians 3:12 (NKJV)
*¹² "In whom we have boldness and access with confidence through **faith** in Him."*

God does not want us to be timid but bold

in our confidence as we put our faith into action.

Jesus gave me a clearer understanding of faith with this acronym:

> **F**ully
> **A**ccepting
> **I**
> **T**rust
> **H**im

It is important we fully accept who Jesus is and to completely trust in Him.

1 John 5:4 (NKJV)
*⁴ "For whatever is born of God overcomes the world. And this is the **victory** that has overcome the world— our **faith**."*

When we begin having this kind of faith, we will experience "**No More Darkness, Only Victory!**"

No More Darkness, Only Victory!

Reflection

Where do you struggle the most in the area of faith?

How BIG is your God? Think about this concept for a bit in order for your reflection to be an honest one.

What areas do you tend to hang onto because you are afraid to let go and let God have complete control?

Describe several ways that God has provided for you, taken care of things, and/or answered your prayers when you weren't sure if He would?

No More Darkness, Only Victory!

Write down some verses that speak to your heart about faith and trusting in God.

Take a moment to pray and ask God to help you have more faith and trust in Him. Ask Him to take away any fear, worry, or anything else that is keeping you from having the type of faith God desires you to have.

AREA TWO: HOPE

Hope is defined as confident trust with the expectation of fulfillment. When I read *1 Corinthians 13:13*, I wondered why hope would be an area that God felt important enough to endure?

For me, hope is a happy word! It provides a ray of sunshine when life around me seems dark and dreary. It is the light at the end of the tunnel. I am saddened by the despair that so many Christians carry as they trudge through life each day. If only they could have hope and learn to place their trust in God, knowing that He can do what He says He will do.

Jeremiah 29:11 (NIV)
*[11] "For I know the plans I have for you," declares the LORD, "plans to prosper you and not to harm you, plans to give you **hope** and a future."*

God is clearly telling us that His plans for us are good and contain hope. They are not disastrous or hopeless. We need to stop dwelling on the negative, half-empty attitude and start dwelling on the positive, half-full attitude.

If we look closely at *Jeremiah 29:11*, we will notice that God has plans for us. Unfortunately, we don't always rely on Him and His plans. As a result, we don't always receive the blessings He has planned for us. One reason so many become hopeless is because we don't allow God to plan our day each and every day. He doesn't make us follow His plans but instead gives us freedom of choice to choose what we want to do every day. When we don't follow His will or plan, we wonder why we experience stress in our lives. Trusting isn't always understanding our circumstances, but trusting in the faithfulness of our Savior who makes all things beautiful in His time. God wants us to trust Him enough to allow Him to direct and guide our lives on a daily basis.

> *Proverbs 3:5-6 (NKJV)*
> *[5] "Trust in the Lord with all your heart, And lean not on your own understanding; [6] In all*

your ways acknowledge Him, And He shall direct your paths."

We can only trust Jesus completely when we know Him intimately.

Psalm 71:5 (NLT)
*⁵ "O Lord, you alone are my **hope**. I've trusted you, O LORD, from childhood."*

God alone is our only true hope. How many times do we turn to anything and everything in our desperate pursuit of hope? It should be no surprise when we come up empty handed feeling hopeless and empty. I have known so many who in their pursuit of hope or fulfillment turn to addictions or other areas of emptiness only to discover they are as hopeless and unfulfilled as ever.

The following verse is such a powerful verse that should allow us to feel a deep sense of peace and hope.

Romans 15:13 (NLT)
*¹³ "I pray that God, the source of **hope**, will fill you completely with joy and peace because you trust in Him. Then you will overflow with confident hope through the power of the Holy Spirit."*

We need to claim this promise today and begin having hope and fulfillment in our lives.

Jesus also promised to provide us with a Comforter, His Holy Spirit. What a vital role the Holy Spirit plays in the area of hope!

John 14:16 (KJV)
¹⁶ "And I will pray to the Father, and He shall give you another Comforter, that He may abide with you forever..."

Jesus promises that the Father has sent us His Spirit, His Holy Spirit, to show us just how much He truly loves us. His Holy Spirit has been sent to be our friend, our counselor, our guide, our comforter, and whatever else we may need at any given moment. This should bring us tremendous hope!

Part of the reason we don't feel comforted is because we don't understand how God actually comforts us. Even though God has given us His tremendous gift of His Spirit, who lives in us, we act as though He is not in us or even with us. We don't allow Him to envelop our lives. Instead we push Him into a small corner of our being and wonder why we feel empty and hopeless. His desire is to saturate and overflow our entire temple (His place of residence) with His Spirit in order to bring us abundant comfort, peace, and hope.

Another reason we don't feel comforted the way God desires is because we sometimes pursue fleshly comfort instead of spiritual comfort. We must understand that the Holy Spirit doesn't comfort us by manipulating our feelings. Our feelings are like a rollercoaster constantly moving up and down. The Holy Spirit provides comfort by bringing us truth that doesn't change. Our comfort should come from what we know to be true, not by what we are feeling.

John 8:32 (NLT)
³² "And you will <u>know</u> the truth, and the truth will set you free."

Our feelings can't set us free because they are never the same, but God's Truth never changes. Hallelujah!

Hebrews 13:8 (NLT)
⁸ "Jesus Christ is the same yesterday, today, and forever."

When we allow Him to fill our temple with His Spirit and allow Him to fill all of our empty places with His truths and His promises, we will truly feel comforted and full of hope. Doesn't this truth spark a bit of hope in your spirit?

As we fully comprehend and allow the Holy Spirit to saturate our temple and not just the corner, we will realize that what He promises us in *1 John 4* is true.

1 John 4:4b (KJV)
^{4b} "...because greater is He that is in you, than he that is in the world."

God is our Victor, our Messiah, our Jehovah, our Comforter, our Healer, and our God. Nothing can compare to Him! Nothing! Hallelujah! Our awesome God lives in us! Praise Him Always!

Romans 5:1-5 (NKJV)
*^{1} "Therefore, having been justified by faith, we have peace with God through our Lord Jesus Christ. ^{2} through whom also we have access by faith into this grace in which we stand, and rejoice in **hope** of the glory of God. ^{3} And not only that, but we also glory in tribulations, knowing that tribulation produces perseverance; ^{4} and perseverance, character; and character, **hope**. ^{5} Now **hope** does not disappoint, because the love of God has been poured out in our hearts by the Holy Spirit who was given to us."*

Because our feelings are sometimes ruled by what is going on around us, we still find hope hard

No More Darkness, Only Victory!

to grasp. When we allow God to rule our hearts, we will begin to find hope. A hope that cannot be measured because it will be overflowing. We will begin to completely understand *"The joy of the Lord is our strength." (Nehemiah 8:10)*

We also walk around without any hope or joy because we are too busy carrying around the heavy burden of lies that Satan has chained to us. We are prisoners of our own choosing, keeping the key hidden that will unlock our chains. Do we unconsciously keep our keys hidden because we have become so accustomed to carrying around our chains and burdens that we can't imagine the possibility of being set free? Regardless, we need to allow Jesus to set us free.

Isaiah 40:31 (NKJV)
³¹ "But those who wait on the Lord shall renew their strength; They shall mount up with wings like eagles, They shall run and not be weary, They shall walk and not faint."

It is imperative that we apply what we are

asked to do in *Isaiah 40:31*. God wants us to let go of our chains and our burdens and wait on Him. When we do this, we will find new strength and will fly on wings like eagles. We will no longer be in the pit of doom, but we will be flying and soaring high as we feel the unleashing freedom of victory. We will run and not get tired. This newly claimed victory should make us begin to feel a spark of **hope and joy**.

Unlock your chains of lies and burdens you have been carrying around for years and start soaring high! The view will be spectacular!

Hebrews 6:19 (NIV)
*[19] "We have this **hope** as an anchor for the soul, firm and secure. It enters the inner sanctuary behind the curtain, where our forerunner, Jesus, has entered on our behalf."*

How appropriate to be writing about **hope** on the anniversary of my sweet and loving mom's Heavenly birthday (November 7th). What a day that had to be for her when she was able to be with her Lord and Savior!

As I was struggling trying to figure out how to refocus my life without my 84 year old mom's example on how to love, to give to others, to sacrifice self for others, etc., I read:

I Peter 1:3-7 (NKJV):
*³ "Blessed be the God and Father of our Lord Jesus Christ, who according to His abundant mercy has begotten us again to a living **hope** through the resurrection of Jesus Christ from the dead, ⁴ to an inheritance incorruptible and undefiled and that does not fade away, reserved in heaven for you, ⁵ who are kept by the power of God through faith for salvation ready to be revealed in the last time. ⁶ In this you greatly rejoice, though now for a little while, if need be, you have been grieved by various trials, ⁷ that the genuineness of your faith, being much more precious than gold that perishes, though it is tested by fire, may be found to praise, honor, and glory at the revelation of Jesus Christ."*

God has given us hope to anchor, not uproot our soul. The anchor is a symbol of God's unchanging word and love. It is hard to have hope if we are allowing Satan to constantly uproot or steer us in the wrong direction in our thoughts and actions. God desires us to anchor ourselves in Him by knowing who He is and knowing in our hearts that He is hope. We need to allow Him to shine His Light into our darkness.

As I was having a pity party for myself, God reminded me to have hope in Him. I asked Him to give me a simple definition of hope since I was obviously having trouble grasping on to His hope. He gave me this simple acronym:

> **H**aving
> **O**nly
> **P**ositive
> **E**xpectations

I had to stop focusing on the negative things surrounding me and on the negative things I was constantly thinking about. I had to turn my eyes to Him, the anchor of my soul (*Hebrews 6:19*).

Yes, I still have struggles in this area, but God is not the author of darkness but of light. When I focus my attention on Him, His Light always outshines the darkness allowing me to anchor onto His HOPE! Praise Him Always!

The following verses speak of the kind of hope that outshines darkness. Anchor onto one of these verses. Carry this verse with you and meditate on it whenever Satan is trying to steer you into darkness and keep you from anchoring to Him, your HOPE!

> *Jeremiah 29:11 (NIV)*
> *¹¹ "For I know the plans I have for you," declares the LORD, "plans to prosper you and not to harm you, plans to give you **hope** and a future."*

> *Isaiah 40:31 (NIV)*
> *³¹ "But those who **hope** in the LORD will renew their strength; They will soar on wings like eagles; they will run and not grow weary, they*

will walk and not be faint."

Hebrews 11:1 (NIV)
*¹ "Now faith is confidence in what we **hope** for and assurance about what we do not see."*

Psalm 119:114 (NIV)
*¹¹⁴ "You are my refuge and my shield; I have put my **hope** in Your Word."*

Hebrews 10:23 (NIV)
*²³ "Let us hold unswervingly to the **hope** we profess, for He who promised is faithful."*

Psalm 31:24 (NIV)
*²⁴ "Be strong and take heart, all you who **hope** in the LORD."*

Romans 8:25 (NIV)
*²⁵ "But if we **hope** for what we do not yet have, we wait for it patiently."*

Romans 5:3–4 (NIV)
³ "Not only so, but we also glory in our sufferings, because we know that suffering produces perseverance; ⁴ perseverance,

*character; and character, **hope**."*

Proverbs 13:12 (NIV)
*¹² "**Hope** deferred makes the heart sick, but a longing fulfilled is a tree of life."*

Psalm 33:22 (NIV)
*²² "May your unfailing love be with us, LORD, as we put our **hope** in You."*

Satan will try over and over to throw us down, to tell us we have no hope, that Jesus is against us, and that Jesus doesn't love us. We know these are all lies, but when we are feeling down and beaten up, it is sometimes easier for us to hang onto some of these lies. Memorize the verses about hope so they will be anchored in your heart to use against Satan whenever he is trying to defeat you, and you will experience "***No More Darkness, Only Victory!***"

Reflection

Write down some of the verses about hope and describe how they can and will help you when you feel you have no hope.

What lies have you been hanging onto that have kept you from experiencing the "hope" God desires for you?

No More Darkness, Only Victory!

What chains has Satan locked around you that keep you from soaring on the wings of an eagle? Remember - the truth will set you free, but you have to be truthful with yourself in order for these chains to be unlocked and released from your life.

Ask God to help you unlock the chains you are dragging around so that you may begin to experience hope and victory.

AREA THREE: LOVE

1 Corinthians 13:13 (NKJV)
*[13] "And now abide faith, hope, **love**, these three; but the greatest of these is love."*

Love is defined as a deep tender affection or devotion to someone. Why is love the greatest of these three? Scripture reveals the answer. Simply put...**God is love**!

1 John 4:8 (NIV)
[8] "Whoever does not love does not know God, because <u>God is love</u>."

Since love is a human emotion going up and down, we must look to the One who possesses perfect love, our Lord and Savior. How does He demonstrate the kind of love we are to have in our lives?

John 3:16a (NIV)
[16a] "For God so loved the world that He gave his one and only Son..."

What an incredible sacrifice God made for us!

He loves us enough to not just give us abundant blessings, but He loves us with a love so strong and so deep that it allowed Him to sacrifice His only Son for us.

Jesus knew without a doubt that He would sacrifice His life for us. His love is so remarkable that it took Him to the cross to be beaten, tortured, and nailed to that cross until He took His last painful breath. He did all of this for you and me. Why? Because He loves us that much!

1 John 3:16a (NIV)
*16a "This is how we know what **love** is: Jesus Christ laid down His life for us..."*

We need to allow God to fill our minds with a true understanding of what love is so that we can begin to experience victory. The only way we can truly comprehend faith and hope is when we comprehend love and allow love to be the driving force in our Christian walk, steering us to the destination of faith and hope.

We cannot love God on a part time basis. God

wants **all** of our love.

Deuteronomy 6:5 (NKJV)
*⁵ "You shall **love** the LORD your God with **all** your heart, with **all** your soul, and with **all** your strength."*

The key word in this verse is the word **all** which is used three times. He wants all of us. We can't just give God lip service, we must love God with everything we have, everything! When we learn to do this, we will begin to love God, others, and ourselves the way God desires us to love.

Love is also the foundation for everything in our spiritual walk. If we don't love God the way He commands, we cannot have faith or hope since they are built on the foundation of love.

Several years ago God revealed a commandment to me in a way that I had never perceived. This commandment is actually mentioned three times in the Bible.

(Leviticus 19:18; Matthew 22:39; James 2:8)
"You shall love your neighbor as yourself."

When I studied this verse, God revealed to me that before I could love anyone else, I had to learn to love myself. I had to look inward and start unveiling all of the things I didn't love or even like about myself and give those areas to God. I had to learn to renounce Satan and his lies about me that I had believed for too long and begin to cover myself with God's promises including:

Psalms 139:14 (NKJV):
^{14} "I will praise You, for I am fearfully and wonderfully made..."

When I was finally able to let go of the lies from Satan that I believed about myself, I was able to begin loving myself the way God desired. As a result, I was also able to love others the way He desired for me to love them.

I know I am not a minority in the area of having to learn to love myself. I have met many Christians who have listened to Satan's lies about themselves for so long that those lies appear to be truths. As a result, many fall into a pit of unworthiness, depression, divorce, low-self esteem, etc. We can only take someone as far as we have gone ourselves; therefore, if we don't love ourselves, we can't possibly love others the way Christ commands us to love.

When I began looking at myself and others through the eyes of Jesus, my vision was no longer blinded by Satan. I am worthy! You are worthy! If we don't believe we are worthy, then we are saying that God made a mistake when He created you and me! We know God NEVER makes mistakes; therefore, we are worthy! Praise Him always!

Learning to love Jesus, myself, and others the way God intended has been one of the most freeing experiences of my life because love truly is the greatest! I want to encourage you to study the Bible concerning love and what God desires for you to learn from His perspective of love. I believe you will find this to be one of the most victorious steps you will take.

This following acronym I wrote sums up Jesus' love for us:

> **L**ord, You are
> **O**ur Savior and
> **V**ictor for
> **E**ternity

Reflection

What areas are you struggling in when it comes to love? Be still and listen to Him as He surrounds you with His abundant love.

Write down the areas that are keeping you from loving "yourself" and then give those areas to God.

What is keeping you from loving "others" the way God desires?

No More Darkness, Only Victory!

Ask God to reveal verses to you that demonstrate the type of love He desires you to have.

CHAPTER 12
"PSALM 23!"

When I was a small child, I remember hearing adults from time to time quoting *Psalm 23*. I also remember being somewhat afraid of the part "walking through the valley of the shadow of death!" I didn't understand the Psalm but knew death was not something I wanted. Fortunately, as time progressed, I grew up both physically and spiritually and *Psalm 23* became and still is one of my favorite passages in the Bible because of the promises the Lord gives us as our Shepherd. Before it became one of my favorites, I had to study it verse by verse to see what our Shepherd really was promising us.

Psalm 23:1 (NKJV)
¹ "The Lord is my shepherd; I shall not want."

Verse one reveals the relationship we as Christians have with Jesus. We are not the shepherd of our lives. God is our Shepherd. He has promised that He will provide, guide, and take care of us. Jesus desires an intimate relationship with us; therefore, He knows our comings and goings (*Psalm 121:8*), He knows the number of hairs on our head (*Luke 12:7*), and He knows when one of us, His sheep, is lost and will seek to find us (*Matthew 18: 12, Luke 15:4*). When we try to take over and shepherd ourselves, our children, and others; we will walk in darkness and out of our Shepherd's protection. However, when we allow Jesus to shepherd our lives, we shall not want because we are allowing Jesus to lead us and to provide for us in ways that only He can provide.

> *Psalm 23:2 (NKJV)*
> *2 "He makes me to lie down in green pastures;*
> *He leads me beside still waters."*

This verse is so descriptive of what Jesus desires us to do during certain times in our lives. When we are weary, He brings us to green pastures - not parched pastures. He desires us here to lie down and rest and know who He is...

our Shepherd. He also leads us beside still waters, not turbulent waters. When we find ourselves in parched pastures and turbulent waters, we need to look to our Shepherd. He is there with us and will lead us out of or through the turbulence if we release control to Him. Once we are through the turbulence, He will make us rest in green pastures and lead us beside the still waters! He allows us to rest so we can then be ready for His next promise.

Psalm 23:3 (NKJV)
³ "He restores my soul; He leads me in the paths of righteousness for His name's sake."

God's desire is for us to bring Him glory. We can do this when we radiate who He is. As a result, He will restore our soul to righteousness and spiritual healing if we allow Him to do so. The concept of "restore" is so powerful but may get lost if we don't pause and understand what Jesus is promising us in this verse. To restore something is to bring it back to its original state. We do not have to be worn down and trampled but can be restored and renewed. Jesus can restore us when we recognize where we are choosing to walk. When we let go and allow our Shepherd to lead us out of turbulence, we can trust that Jesus will begin to restore our soul. Jesus will restore us and then lead us, but only **if** we are willing to follow Him in righteousness for His name's sake.

> *Psalm 23:4 (NKJV)*
> *⁴ "Yea, though I walk through the valley of the shadow of death, I will fear no evil; For You are with me; Your rod and Your staff, they comfort me."*

At times we will encounter danger and heartache in our lives, but He tells us to not fear because He is with us. Remember, that fear in and of itself is partly due to lack of faith. Do you believe that Jesus, your Shepherd, is with you? We can't go very far in our spiritual journey if we don't grasp and believe this promise. God will "never" leave us nor forsake us (*Deuteronomy 31:6*). His rod not only protects us, but may need to be used to bring us back to Him if we stray from His protection. His staff is representative of who we choose to lean on and trust. God is our staff and our strength. We can always lean on Him for support as we allow His rod and staff to protect us from ourselves and from our enemies.

Psalm 23:5 (NKJV)
⁵ "You prepare a table before me in the presence of my enemies; You anoint my head with oil: My cup runs over."

This is a beautiful picture of peace and tranquility. We know the enemy will forever be present in our lives, but we don't have to allow the enemy to invade. Jesus prepares a table for us in order to give us hope. The prepositional phrase "in the presence of my enemies" lets us know He is there with us in the storm. He demonstrates through the preparation of His table that regardless of our circumstances, He is always taking care of our needs. He doesn't care where we are or who we are. He only cares that we come to the table He has prepared for us. When we come to His table and allow Him to be our Savior and our Shepherd, He will anoint us with His Holy Spirit. When a shepherd anointed the sheep's head with oil, it protected them from flies, ticks, lice, and other parasites. Our Shepherd, Jesus, anoints us with His Spirit to protect us from the parasites of the world. Finally, our cup will run over as God continually pours His abundant blessings into our lives. Pause for a moment and meditate on this promise as it envelops your fears and thoughts.

Psalm 23:6 (NKJV)
⁶ "Surely goodness and mercy shall follow me all the days of my life: and I will dwell in the house of the Lord forever."

I love the final verse of *Psalm 23* because of the promise that goodness and mercy will be with us every day. Jesus wants our lives to be filled with His goodness and His mercy in order to show us how much He truly loves us and desires to bless us. As His children, He promises us that we will dwell with Him forever and ever! We can rest in hope that regardless of what happens in this world discouragement, depression, divorce, death, etc., we will be with our Shepherd for eternity.

Psalm 23 is a chapter that should calm our spirit and encourage us when we realize that Jesus is the GOOD SHEPHERD and HE is ours for eternity! Praise Him always!

Reflection

What areas are you afraid of as you encounter your valley?

No More Darkness, *Only Victory!*

Do you allow Jesus to be your Shepherd? If not, where are you trying to lead?

Study *Psalm 23* and allow it to change the direction of your life as you allow Jesus the Shepherd to lead you and to protect you!

Chapter 13
I "AM"!

In our spiritual journey, it is imperative that we learn as much as we can about the **One** who can set us free from **darkness**, and who can allow us to experience **victory** in our lives.

We need to focus on the name God gives Himself... "**I AM**". There are seven "I AM" statements in John's Gospel.

- **First, I AM the BREAD of LIFE!**

    John 6:35 (NLT)
    *35 Jesus replied, "**I AM the bread of life**. Whoever comes to Me will never be hungry again. Whoever believes in Me will never be thirsty."*

John 6 starts out with Jesus performing the miracle of feeding the five thousand with five loaves of bread and two fish. After feeding the crowd, Jesus went to the hills to be alone. Later that evening the disciples decided to take the boat and cross over to Capernaum. They had only rowed a few miles when a strong wind swept the sea making the sea extremely rough. With no boat to get into, Jesus began walking on the water to get to the disciples. When He approached them, He told them to not be afraid since He was there. The disciples eagerly let Jesus into the boat, and they arrived safely at their destination.

The next day, the crowds followed Jesus to Capernaum to look for Him. When He noticed that they were only seeking Him because He had fed them, He began telling them about the true bread from Heaven and not the perishable bread.

John 6:35-50 (NLT)
[35] Jesus replied, "I am the bread of life. Whoever comes to Me will never be hungry again. Whoever believes in Me will never be thirsty. [36] But you haven't believed in Me even though you have seen Me. [37] However, those the Father has given Me will come to Me, and I will never reject them. [38] For I have come

down from heaven to do the will of God who sent Me, not to do My own will. ³⁹ And this is the will of God, that I should not lose even one of all those He has given me, but that I should raise them up at the last day. ⁴⁰ For it is My Father's will that all who see His Son and believe in Him should have eternal life. I will raise them up at the last day."

⁴¹ Then the people began to murmur in disagreement because He had said, "I am the bread that came down from heaven." ⁴² They said, "Isn't this Jesus, the son of Joseph? We know His father and mother. How can He say, 'I came down from heaven'?"

⁴³ But Jesus replied, "Stop complaining about what I said. ⁴⁴ For no one can come to Me unless the Father who sent Me draws them to Me, and at the last day I will raise them up. ⁴⁵ As it is written in the Scriptures, 'They will all be taught by God.' Everyone who listens to the Father and learns from Him comes to Me. ⁴⁶ (Not that anyone has ever seen the Father;

> only I, Who was sent from God, have seen Him.)
> ⁴⁷ "I tell you the truth, anyone who believes has eternal life. ⁴⁸ Yes, **I am the bread of life**! ⁴⁹ Your ancestors ate manna in the wilderness, but they all died. ⁵⁰ Anyone who eats the bread from heaven, however, will never die."

Jesus is the bread of life. We may need food to keep us alive on this earth, but we need Jesus to live for eternity. When we believe in Him and allow His Word to feed us, we will have eternal life.

- **Second, I AM the LIGHT of the WORLD!**

> John 8:12 (NLT)
> ¹² Jesus spoke to the people once more and said, "**I AM** the light of the world. If you follow Me, you won't have to walk in darkness, because you will have the light that leads to life."

What is the difference between physical light and spiritual light? Physical light is what we notice around us. It is a flashlight or a light bulb or the sunlight, etc. While physical light is good and penetrates darkness and is necessary for plant growth and other vegetation, it does not provide eternal life. Spiritual light is the true light of Jesus. Spiritual light will reveal His Truth, His Word, and His ability to provide us with salvation for eternal life.

If we follow Jesus and accept Him as our Savior, His light will penetrate the darkness in our hearts and will lead us to eternal life. We no longer have to walk in darkness.

John 8:12 reminds me of the traditional song I used to sing as a child and still sing as an adult...

"This Little Light of Mine"

This little light of mine, I'm gonna let it shine.
This little light of mine, I'm gonna let it shine.
This little light of mine, I'm gonna let it shine.
Let it shine, shine, shine. Let it shine!
Everywhere I go, I'm gonna let it shine.
Everywhere I go, I'm gonna let it shine.

Everywhere I go, I'm gonna let it shine.

Let it shine, shine, shine. Let it shine!

Since Jesus, the Light, lives in us when we receive Him as our Savior, we need to let His "Light" shine through us. After all, we have an "Eternal Light" that never goes dark! Praise the Lord!

- **Third, I AM the GATE!**

John 10:9 (NLT)
*⁹ "Yes, **I AM** the gate. Those who come in through Me will be saved. They will come and go freely and will find good pastures."*

When we look at Scripture, we see the important role the shepherd had in keeping his flock safe from predators. We can see the similarities between the sheeps' shepherd and our Shepherd.

Sheep were totally dependent upon their shepherd who was their provider, protector, guide, and companion. The bond between the shepherd and his sheep was so close that the sheep knew and followed their shepherd's voice. Shepherds were inseparable from their flocks. The shepherd would lead his sheep to safe places to graze and to rest. When nightfall approached, the shepherd would lead his sheep to the protection of a pen. This pen was usually made of rock but sometimes the pen did not have a gate. As a result, once the sheep were safe in the pen, the shepherd would lay across the opening of the pen and be the gate to keep predators out, allowing the sheep to be safe.

Jesus is our Shepherd who is our continual gate that protects us from harm. We know Satan will try to devour our lives any way and anywhere he can. He will attack our marriages, our family, our children, our jobs, our health, our finances, our friends, our thoughts, our security, our relationship with Jesus and so many other areas. We can only be protected when we allow Jesus our Shepherd to open and close the gate as He sees fit. After all, He is the Shepherd and is the only one who knows what danger is lurking beyond the boundaries He has placed around us.

Jesus is also the gate to our eternal life. We can only get to our eternal home through Jesus' gate. We have enternal security in Jesus.

> *John 10:9 (NLT)*
> *⁹ "Yes, **I am** the gate. <u>Those who come in through Me will be saved</u>. They will come and go freely and will find good pastures."*

We all struggle with fear and doubt, but we need to truly understand what Jesus is promising us. He is the gate that can only be opened by Him. When we believe in who He is and pass through His gate, we are saved. He will never leave us nor forsake us (*Hebrews 13:5*)!

> *John 10:27-30 (NKJV)*
> *²⁷ "My sheep hear My voice, and I know them, and they follow Me. ²⁸ And I give them eternal life, and they shall never perish; neither shall anyone snatch them out of My hand. ²⁹ My Father, who has given them to Me, is greater*

than all; and no one is able to snatch them out of My Father's hand. ³⁰ I and My Father are one."

Pause and meditate on these verses. Notice everything our Shepherd is providing us: our intimate relationship with Him, eternal life, His constant protection, and His eternal love.

- **Fourth, I AM the GOOD SHEPHERD!**

John 10:14-15 (NLT)
*¹⁴ "<u>**I AM** the good shepherd</u>; I know My own sheep, and they know Me, ¹⁵ just as My Father knows Me and I know the Father. So I sacrifice My life for the sheep."*

Jesus is "<u>the</u> Good" Shepherd. Jesus uses the definite article "the" because He isn't just "a" shepherd, but He is "the" Shepherd. Therefore, in using the phrase "the Good Shepherd," Jesus is referring to His inherent goodness and His righteousness. He knows each one of us on an intimate level by knowing what we desire, what we think, what we need, etc. His relationship with us is so important that as our Good Shepherd, He sacrificed His life for us. This demonstrates how much He loves us, His sheep. Jesus showed us His love by leaving heaven, entering humanity, living a perfect life, and paying the price for our sins by sacrificing His life on the cross. He truly is "The Good Shepherd!"

- **Fifth, I AM the RESURRECTION and the LIFE!**

John 11:25 (NLT)
*²⁵ Jesus told her, "<u>**I AM** the resurrection and the life</u>. Anyone who believes in Me will live, even after dying."*

There is no resurrection or eternal life apart from Christ. The resurrection of Jesus is so important in our lives as Christians because it proves who Jesus stated He was - the Messiah, the Savior of the World! He has the power to overcome death! Jesus does more than give life because He is life: therefore, death has no power over Him. As believers, it is reassuring to know that Jesus bestows this spiritual life on those of us who believe in Him. We also know that as believers, we will experience resurrection because of the eternal life Jesus gives to us. As a result, it is impossible for death to defeat us.

At one point in my life, I was scared of dying because I wasn't sure what happened to us when we died. As I continued to study the Bible, I saw that with Christians there is no death. We go immediately from this earthly dwelling to our Heavenly dwelling.

2 Corinthians 5:8 (NLT)
⁸ "Yes, we are fully confident, and we would rather be away from these earthly bodies, for then we will be at home with the Lord!"

It is comforting to know we are never separated from Jesus, never! Praise the Lord!

- **Sixth, I AM the WAY, the TRUTH, and the LIFE!**

John 14:6 (NLT)
*⁶ Jesus told him, "**I AM** <u>the way, the truth, and</u>*

<u>the life</u>. *No one can come to the Father except through Me."*

Jesus used the definite article to distinguish Himself in all three areas. The reason for this is because He is **the** Only Way, **the** Only Truth, and **the** Only Life!

- The Way – Jesus is <u>**the only way**</u> to heaven. There is no other way to heaven or to the Father except through Jesus.

Acts 4:12 (NLT)
[12] "There is salvation in no one else! God has given no other name under heaven by which we must be saved."

- The Truth – Jesus is **the only truth** we need to know and believe.

John 1:1 (NLT)
[1] "In the beginning the Word already existed. The Word was with God, and the Word was God."

- The Life - Jesus is **the only life** to follow in

order for us to live eternally with Him.

John 14:19 (NLT)
[19] "Soon the world will no longer see Me, but you will see Me. Since I live, you also will live."

- **Seventh, I AM the TRUE GRAPEVINE!**

John 15:1 (NLT)
*[1] "**I AM** <u>the true grapevine</u>, and my Father is the gardener."*

We (the branches) are connected to Jesus (the vine), and when we obey His commandments, we will bear fruit; therefore, glorifying God (the gardener). Jesus truly desires for us to have a relationship with Him; therefore, He wants us to always stay connected to Him (the vine). We can do this when we recognize who He is and how much He loves us and how much He sacrificed for us. Remembering our relationship with Our Lord and Savior is key to our eternal life and victory in Him.

There are two words we need to remember

about our Lord and Savior "I AM!" He is without a doubt the great "I AM!" Get into the habit of saying "I AM" concerning areas you are praying about. Example: When praying for healing, remember Jesus will answer, "I AM the healer." When praying for salvation, remember Jesus will answer, "I AM the Savior." In everything and everywhere, He is and will always be: "**I AM**!".

I wrote a poem about who Jesus is.

"YOU ARE"

You are our **Wonderful Counselor** guiding us along the way.
Making sure we have Your directions each and every day.
You give us advice in Your Word as we learn more about You,
Knowing that everything You tell us is always real and true.

You are our **Mighty God** from the beginning to the end,
You know all there is to know which is hard for

us to comprehend.
You take care of our every burden and uphold us with Your hands,
As we trust in Your strength and power for all You have planned.

You are our **Everlasting Father** who has given us eternal life,
You help us through every situation and every little strife.
You love us now and forever no matter what we may do,
To spend eternity with our Father as we give our lives to You.

You are our **Prince of Peace** who can calm our every fear,
As You teach us to let go - knowing You are here.
You can calm the stormy waters as they come our way,
All we have to do is to lean on You each and every day!
Amen!

I wrote an acronym for our "relationship" with Him:

> **R**ealizing
> **E**ternity
> **L**ies
> **A**lways
> **T**hrough the Great
> **I** AM.
> **O**ur
> **N**eed for our
> **S**avior's
> **H**and in our lives
> **I**s
> **P**aramount!

Reflection

What is keeping you from realizing and receiving that God is your great **I AM**?

For the next seven days, write down one **I AM** verse for each day and pray this verse into your life.

Raelene Hudson

Day One

Day Two

Day Three

Day Four

No More Darkness, Only Victory!

Day Five

Day Six

Day Seven

Chapter 14
His Amazing Resurrection!

Springtime is one of my favorite times of the year because of the new life that is happening all around us. Trees are budding, flowers are blooming, birds are chirping, grass is growing, the temperature is warming up and on and on. None of this new life would be possible without our Creator's hands!

Psalm 19:1-2 (NIV)
¹ "The heavens declare the glory of God; the skies proclaim the work of His hands. ² Day after day they pour forth speech; night after night they reveal knowledge."

How **Amazing**!

During this season, I often feel as if I am given a new start in areas of my life which makes me feel closer to the Lord. While many choose to do spring cleaning around the house, Jesus also desires us to do spring cleaning in our spiritual lives. He desires us to get rid of things that are preventing Him from planting new seeds in our lives. He wants us to pull out all of the weeds and remove the rocks in our lives that would choke out any new life. His goal is to plant new seeds in our lives that will take root and blossom. **Amazing**!

There are so many areas we take for granted and don't see the details of our Lord at work. Notice the following verses that reveal how those around Jesus were "amazed" at what He did.

- <u>Jesus' victory over doubt and defeat</u>.

    Luke 5:8-10 (NLT)
    *⁸ "When Simon Peter realized what had happened, he fell to his knees before Jesus and said, 'Oh, Lord, please leave me—I'm such a sinful man.' ⁹ For he was awestruck (**amazed**) by the number of fish they had caught, as were the others with him. ¹⁰ His partners, James and John, the sons of Zebedee, were also **amazed**.*

Jesus replied to Simon, 'Don't be afraid! From now on you'll be fishing for people!'"

Matthew 12:22-23 (NLT)
*²² "Then a demon-possessed man, who was blind and couldn't speak, was brought to Jesus. He healed the man so that he could both speak and see. ²³ The crowd was **amazed** and asked, Could it be that Jesus is the Son of David, the Messiah?'"*

- <u>Jesus' teaching</u>.

Mark 1:22 (NLT)
*²² "The people were **amazed** at his teaching, for He taught with real authority—quite unlike the teachers of religious law."*

- <u>Jesus casts out a demon</u>.

Luke 4:36 (NLT)
*³⁶ **Amazed**, the people exclaimed, "What authority and power this man's words possess! Even evil spirits obey Him, and they flee at His command!"*

No More Darkness, Only Victory!

- <u>Jesus heals many people</u>.

   Matthew 15:30-31 (NLT)
   *³⁰ "A vast crowd brought to Him people who were lame, blind, crippled, those who couldn't speak, and many others. They laid them before Jesus, and He healed them all. ³¹ The crowd was **amazed**! Those who hadn't been able to speak were talking, the crippled were made well, the lame were walking, and the blind could see again! And they praised the God of Israel."*

- <u>Jesus calms the storm</u>.

   Matthew 8:23-27 (NLT)
   ²³ "Then Jesus got into the boat and started across the lake with His disciples. ²⁴ Suddenly, a fierce storm struck the lake, with waves breaking into the boat. But Jesus was sleeping. ²⁵ The disciples went and woke Him up, shouting, 'Lord, save us! We're going to drown!' ²⁶ Jesus responded, 'Why are you afraid? You have so little faith!' Then He got up and

*rebuked the wind and waves, and suddenly there was a great calm. [27] The disciples were **amazed**. 'Who is this man?' they asked. 'Even the winds and waves obey Him!'"*

There are so many things that prove how **amazing** our Lord Jesus is! I like to get up early and watch the sunrise. The colors explode across the sky as the sun greets the morning clouds. Every day God paints a new canvas for our enjoyment and wonder. He is an **amazing** God who is truly worthy of our praise! He is **amazing** in power, love, beauty, and intelligence. We cannot fathom the depths of Who He is, yet He invites us to collaborate and fellowship with Him. He longs for us to seek Him. He patiently waits through our mistakes and wanderings. I am so grateful for His incredible love and also for the opportunity to serve such an **amazing** God!

Spring is also a time when we are blessed to see God's flowers begin to bloom. It is amazing to see the intricate details of each flower. Each flower is different and beautiful. I often wonder why God made so many different varieties of flowers with so many details and beauty? Then it dawned on me...every time we look at a flower, we should be reminded of how beautiful God created each one of us. Just like the flowers, God made each one of us different and unique in our own way. **Amazing** isn't it?

When I began thinking about Christ's amazing Resurrection, I thought of the flower and its journey. We are blessed with its beauty for a season but in order for a new flower to bloom the following year, it must die in order to produce seed for new life.

John 12:24 (NLT)
²⁴ "I tell you the truth, unless a kernel of wheat is planted in the soil and dies, it remains alone. But its death will produce many new kernels—a plentiful harvest of new lives."

There can be no resurrection without death. In order to fulfill scripture, Jesus had to die on the cross in order to be resurrected to life eternal.

Easter is one of my favorite holidays because we are allowed to celebrate our RISEN KING! We also get to celebrate our resurrected lives and the continual resurrection that is taking place all around us! Now that is **AMAZING**!

I wrote the following poem in 2001 but wanted to include it as we continually remember there really is: "***No More Darkness, Only Victory!***"

"The Ultimate Sacrifice"

Twas the night before Your crucifixion and all through the land,
No one knew Your inner heart or the greatest of all commands.
You went to the Garden of Gethsemane and prayed that this cup might be done away,
You warned Your disciples to not sleep but to keep watch and to pray.

We all know the outcome as You prayed that God's will would be done,
Your disciples couldn't stay awake, and You were delivered to the evil ones.

No More Darkness, *Only Victory!*

Oh Lord, thank You for giving "The Ultimate Sacrifice,"
In order for us to have eternal life.

We can never know the separation that You surely felt,
When upon that rough and lonely cross You were savagely nailed.
But even during that time you looked down at Your tormentors and said,
"Forgive them Father, because for even them I have bled!"

Conclusion

Not long ago as I said my night time prayers, I was praying earnestly for those affected by Hurricane Harvey, Hurricane Irma, Hurricane Nathan, the fires in Montana and California, the shootings in Las Vegas, and other areas of calamity. I asked God to give me discernment in how to pray or to be receptive to whatever He desired. That night I had the most vivid dream I have had in a long time.

My dream...I was leading a women's life group and needed to leave early to take my dad to a doctor's appointment. The life group was meeting in a new location so I wasn't familiar with the roads. It was storming with high winds and a torrential downpour. It was hard to see through the downpour as I drove on unfamiliar dirt roads in the dark. I rolled down my window and tried to peer out to see what was ahead. As I turned a corner, my car lost control and careened over a cliff. The car turned upside down, and I fell out of the car window plummeting head first to the ground. As I was free falling, I felt a calming peace and told Jesus how much I loved Him. Before I hit the ground, I was gently righted and placed feet first onto the ground. When I glanced forward, there was a gentle looking man with brown hair, dressed in all white looking at me. When I looked into his face he said one thing, **"JOHN 17 verse 1."**

I woke from my dream.

When I got out of bed, I went to my Bible and read the verse from my dream.

John 17:1 (NKJV)
¹ Jesus spoke these words, lifted up His eyes to Heaven, and said: "Father, the hour has come, Glorify Your Son, that Your Son also may glorify You."

I honestly believe God revealed this verse to me in my dream because the hour has come when we need to get back on track and humble ourselves and GLORIFY our LORD and SAVIOR!

God's promise to us is that we can have "**No More Darkness, Only Victory**" when we **GLORIFY HIM** in **ALL** we do.

Let us pray:

Oh Father in Heaven, how we praise Your name! May we know with certainty that You are the LIGHT of this dark world. May we truly seek You first each and every day and dwell on Your wisdom and steadfast promises. May we have discernment and recognize the lies and snares of Satan that he places all around us to cause us to stumble and to walk in defeat. Guide us to Your Truth as we meditate on Your Word. Put Your full Armor of protection over us daily to protect us from the fiery darts of Satan. Help us to love You, ourselves, and others the way You desire. Help us to abide in You, the True Vine, and walk in Your light where there is "**No More Darkness, Only Victory!**" May You bless us abundantly as we give You ALL the glory! Amen!

It is my prayer that we all experience Victory

in our lives as we live For Him. My final acronym:

>**V**ictory
>**I**s
>**C**hrist
>**T**otally
>**O**vercoming and being
>**R**econciled in
>**Y**ou

My son, Garris, shared the following letter he found with our church. I wanted to include it because of the "victorious" message it reveals:

Introduction

The words you are about to experience are true. For they come from the very heart of God. He loves YOU. And He is the Father you have been looking for all your life. This is His love letter to you.

My Child,

You may not know me, but I know everything about you. (*Psalm 139:1*)

I know when you sit down and when you rise up. (*Psalm 139:2*)
I am familiar with all your ways. (*Psalm 139:3*)
Even the very hairs on your head are numbered. (*Matthew 10:29-31*)
For you were made in my image. (*Genesis 1:27*)
In me you live and move and have your being. (*Acts 17:28*)
For you are my offspring. (*Acts 17:28*)
I knew you even before you were conceived. (*Jeremiah 1:4-5*)
I chose you when I planned creation. (*Ephesians 1:11-12*)
You were not a mistake, for all your days are written in my book. (*Psalm 139:15-16*)
I determined the exact time of your birth and where you would live. (*Acts 17:26*)
You are fearfully and wonderfully made. (*Psalm 139:14*)
I knit you together in your mother's womb. (*Psalm 139:13*)
And brought you forth on the day you were born.

No More Darkness, Only Victory!

(*Psalm 71:6*)

I have been misrepresented by those who don't know me. (*John 8:41-44*)

I am not distant and angry, but am the complete expression of love. (*1 John 4:16*)

And it is my desire to lavish my love on you. (*1 John 3:1*)

Simply because you are my child and I am your Father. (*1 John 3:1*)

I offer you more than your earthly father ever could. (*Matthew 7:11*)

For I am the perfect father. (*Matthew 5:48*)

Every good gift that you receive comes from my hand. (*James 1:17*)

For I am your provider and I meet all your needs. (*Matthew 6:31-33*)

My plan for your future has always been filled with hope. (*Jeremiah 29:11*)

Because I love you with an everlasting love. (*Jeremiah 31:3*)

My thoughts toward you are countless as the sand on the seashore. (*Psalm 139:17-18*)

I know when you sit down and when you rise up. (*Psalm 139:2*)
I am familiar with all your ways. (*Psalm 139:3*)
Even the very hairs on your head are numbered. (*Matthew 10:29-31*)
For you were made in my image. (*Genesis 1:27*)
In me you live and move and have your being. (*Acts 17:28*)
For you are my offspring. (*Acts 17:28*)
I knew you even before you were conceived. (*Jeremiah 1:4-5*)
I chose you when I planned creation. (*Ephesians 1:11-12*)
You were not a mistake, for all your days are written in my book. (*Psalm 139:15-16*)
I determined the exact time of your birth and where you would live. (*Acts 17:26*)
You are fearfully and wonderfully made. (*Psalm 139:14*)
I knit you together in your mother's womb. (*Psalm 139:13*)
And brought you forth on the day you were born.

No More Darkness, Only Victory!

(*Psalm 71:6*)

I have been misrepresented by those who don't know me. (*John 8:41-44*)

I am not distant and angry, but am the complete expression of love. (*1 John 4:16*)

And it is my desire to lavish my love on you. (*1 John 3:1*)

Simply because you are my child and I am your Father. (*1 John 3:1*)

I offer you more than your earthly father ever could. (*Matthew 7:11*)

For I am the perfect father. (*Matthew 5:48*)

Every good gift that you receive comes from my hand. (*James 1:17*)

For I am your provider and I meet all your needs. (*Matthew 6:31-33*)

My plan for your future has always been filled with hope. (*Jeremiah 29:11*)

Because I love you with an everlasting love. (*Jeremiah 31:3*)

My thoughts toward you are countless as the sand on the seashore. (*Psalm 139:17-18*)

And I rejoice over you with singing. (*Zephaniah 3:17*)

I will never stop doing good to you. (*Jeremiah 32:40*)

For you are my treasured possession. (*Exodus 19:5*)

I desire to establish you with all my heart and all my soul. (*Jeremiah 32:41*)

And I want to show you great and marvelous things. (*Jeremiah 33:3*)

If you seek me with all your heart, you will find me. (*Deuteronomy 4:29*)

Delight in me and I will give you the desires of your heart. (*Psalm 37:4*)

For it is I who gave you those desires. (*Philippians 2:13*)

I am able to do more for you than you could possibly imagine. (*Ephesians 3:20*)

For I am your greatest encourager. (*2 Thessalonians 2:16-17*)

I am also the Father who comforts you in all your troubles. (*2 Corinthians 1:3-4*)

No More Darkness, Only Victory!

When you are brokenhearted, I am close to you. (*Psalm 34:18*)

As a shepherd carries a lamb, I have carried you close to my heart. (*Isaiah 40:11*)

One day I will wipe away every tear from your eyes. (*Revelation 21:3-4*)

And I'll take away all the pain you have suffered on this earth. (*Revelation 21:3-4*)

I am your Father, and I love you even as I love my son, Jesus. (*John 17:23*)

For in Jesus, my love for you is revealed. (*John 17:26*)

He is the exact representation of my being. (*Hebrews 1:3*)

He came to demonstrate that I am for you, not against you. (*Romans 8:31*)

And to tell you that I am not counting your sins. (*2 Corinthians 5:18-19*)

Jesus died so that you and I could be reconciled. (*2 Corinthians 5:18-19*)

His death was the ultimate expression of my love for you. (*1 John 4:10*)

I gave up everything I loved that I might gain your love. (*Romans 8:31-32*)

If you receive the gift of my son Jesus, you receive me. (*1 John 2:23*)

And nothing will ever separate you from my love again. (*Romans 8:38-39*)

Come home and I'll throw the biggest party heaven has ever seen. (*Luke 15:7*)

I have always been Father, and will always be Father. (*Ephesians 3:14-15*)

My question is...Will you be my child? (*John 1:12-13*)

I am waiting for you. (*Luke 15:11-32*)

Love, Your Dad. Almighty God[1]

---

[1] © 1999 Father Heart Communications - FathersLoveLetter.com

"Only Victory"

No more darkness, only victory you say,
We can have this if only we would faithfully pray.
Pray to You our Christ and King,
Our Lord and Savior who can do anything.

Why is our faith in You so small,
When You, Oh Lord, are the Savior of all?
We take over so many things in our life,
And groan and complain when we encounter strife.

Help us to seek You first in all we do,
Crushing Satan's lies and holding on to what is true.
No more darkness, only victory You say,
Help us to claim this promise today!

By: Raelene Hudson (2017)

SPECIAL NOTE FROM THE AUTHOR:

It is my prayer that you received guidance from this book and will apply *1 Corinthians 10:31* in your lives on a daily basis.

> *"Therefore, whether you eat or drink, or whatever you do, do ALL to the glory of God."*

I pray that your journey with Christ will allow you to take the necessary steps to consistently experience "***No More Darkness, Only Victory!***"

Printed in the USA
CPSIA information can be obtained
at www.ICGtesting.com
LVHW090400140924
790893LV00002B/433

9 781034 544500